GREAT LIVES OBSERVED

Gerald Emanuel Stearn, *General Editor*

EACH VOLUME IN THE SERIES VIEWS THE CHARACTER AND ACHIEVEMENT OF A GREAT WORLD FIGURE IN THREE PERSPECTIVES—THROUGH HIS OWN WORDS, THROUGH THE OPINIONS OF HIS CONTEMPORARIES, AND THROUGH RETROSPECTIVE JUDGMENTS—THUS COMBINING THE INTIMACY OF AUTOBIOGRAPHY, THE IMMEDIACY OF EYEWITNESS OBSERVATION, AND THE OBJECTIVITY OF MODERN SCHOLARSHIP.

ADRIENNE KOCH, *the editor of this volume in the Great Lives Observed series, is Professor of History at the University of Maryland. She has written several books on Jefferson, Madison, and the other major founding fathers. Professor Koch has also edited numerous volumes on the early Americn philosophers-statesmen, including the recent publication of her* The American Enlightenment.

GREAT LIVES OBSERVED

Jefferson

Edited by ADRIENNE KOCH

*I consider him the most powerful advocate
democracy has ever had.*

—Tocqueville

*The principles of Jefferson are the
definitions and axioms of free society.*

—Lincoln

68943

A SPECTRUM BOOK

PRENTICE-HALL, INC., ENGLEWOOD CLIFFS, N. J.

To my husband, Larry Kegan

Current printing (last number): 10 9 8 7 6 5 4 3 2 1

C–13-509810-6

P–13-509802-5

Library of Congress Catalog Card Number: 75–133052

Printed in the United States of America

PRENTICE-HALL INTERNATIONAL, INC. (*London*)
PRENTICE-HALL OF AUSTRALIA, PTY. LTD. (*Sydney*)
PRENTICE-HALL OF CANADA, LTD. (*Toronto*)
PRENTICE-HALL OF INDIA PRIVATE LIMITED (*New Delhi*)
PRENTICE-HALL OF JAPAN, INC. (*Tokyo*)

Contents

PART ONE
JEFFERSON LOOKS AT THE WORLD

/1

2

Preamble from a Bill for the More General Diffusion of
Knowledge, *20*   An Act for Establishing Religious Freedom,
20

3

On the Law "To Diffuse Knowledge More Generally
Through the Mass of the People," *24*   On the Freedom of
Religion, *26*   On Slavery, *27*   On Manufactures, *28*

4

Mission to Europe and the Ethics of Public Trust, *32*   Evils
of Confederation, *33*   "One Nation Only," *34*   "A Crusade
Against Ignorance," *34*   "A Little Rebellion Now and

v

GREAT LIVES OBSERVED

JEFFERSON

Introduction

In April of 1962, President John F. Kennedy was entertaining the Nobel Laureates at the White House with a dinner in their honor. In a genial moment he turned to the impressive assemblage and said with a grin that he saw before him "probably the greatest concentration of talent and genius in this house except for perhaps those times when Thomas Jefferson ate alone."

Few men have been foolish enough to deny in their hearts what they may have denied with their lips: that Jefferson, in the brilliant reach of his mind and the limitless play of his interests, was one of the most gifted men ever to assume the tasks of democratic statesmanship. The historian, Henry Steele Commager, attempting to assess Jefferson's mighty influence over his countrymen, from the opening act of Independence to our present point in history, wrote: "Jefferson is the central figure in American history and—if freedom and democracy survive in our generation—he may yet prove to be the central figure of modern history." The philosopher, John Dewey, hailed Jefferson as "the first modern to state in human terms the principles of democracy." The great French sociologist, Alexis de Tocqueville, in his classic work, *Democracy in America,* stated without qualification: "I consider him the most powerful advocate democracy has ever had."

The young Virginian who became the symbol of America's most compelling ideals—so conclusively that *both* sides in every heated substantive policy from Jefferson's days to ours have claimed the sanction of his principles—was himself of the belief that politics *per se* was an inferior form of human life. His democratic faith, so properly coupled with the ideals he wrote into the Declaration of Independence, the human rights of equality, of life, liberty, and the pursuit of happiness, was the faith of a humanist who had put himself to school in the method of the experimental sciences. Thus his comprehensive program was to establish a new social-political experiment, a democratic modern republic. Its base would be free men using their intelligence and information to play a responsible part, directly or indirectly, in the significant decisions of government. But the fruits and results of a democratic republic were what he valued, not political power or political

Adapted from Adrienne Koch, *The American Enlightenment* (New York: George Braziller, Inc., 1965), pp. 277–85.

form in themselves. The chance to learn, to engage in enlightened discourse and debate, to work with some pride in a suitable task, to cultivate friendships, and enter the many-mansioned realm of art and culture as more than passive recipients, to quest endlessly, creatively, for the meanings of life, to win ever more of the inexhaustible truth—these were the moral goods for which free men would gratefully endure the burdens of self-government. So often is Jefferson cited as an "apostle of liberty"—as though liberty could be spoken for without questions for *how, by what means, at what cost,* and *through what work, courage,* and *sacrifice*—that it is essential to remember that he had no illusions that liberty was absolute and undivided! Not a cheap and easy liberty to which men are "transported in a featherbed," but the liberty which is the obverse side of responsibility, of intelligent concern and planning, and which at best ascends to a general rule, never to a universal dogma.

Since Jefferson was the child of the European Enlightenment and in himself the superb fulfillment of the American Enlightenment, one must consider the underlying assumptions of his liberal social views. Long before Marx formulated the slogan that the role of philosophers was not merely to understand the world but to change it, Jefferson had come, through his own process of growth and through the selective affiliation with philosophers he would regard as his ideals, to link theory and action, ideals and reality, principles and practice. As a youth in Western Virginia, he was under the tutelage of his father, Peter Jefferson, a self-made man, a surveyor, cartographer, and skilled craftsman who had himself built the house at Shadwell on the farm where Jefferson was born. Jefferson's memories of his boyhood included less about his mother who came of good aristocratic Randolph stock, than of his father who taught him how to ride, manage a canoe, do carpentry and building, manage a farm, shoot, plant, judge livestock. His father died when Jefferson was fourteen years old, leaving a legacy of some 1400 acres to his son; and yet the fact that his father had arranged that the boy be given a complete training in the classics was mentioned in Jefferson's *Autobiography* in this way: "I thank on my knees him who directed my early education, for having put into my possession this rich source of delight; and I would not exchange it for anything which I could then have acquired."

To this classical training, he soon added intensive exploration of the new world of natural science and mathematics, under the instruction of Dr. William Small at William and Mary College. Praised by Jefferson as "the most excellent Small," revered ever after as his beloved teacher, this professor of natural philosophy had been responsible for purchasing scientific apparatus for the college which has been described as "at least comparable to what Harvard then possessed." He also built up a library on scientific experiments and inventions for the college. Before this enlightened Scotsman returned to England, he had made a daily companion of young Jefferson, and was responsible for introducing him to George Wythe, with whom Jefferson studied law for five years after college. Small and Wythe were also the men who conducted Jefferson into the intimate circle of friends who visited with Governor Fauquier at the Palace in Williamsburg. To their common interest in the advance of science, and the principles of law and government, these men joined the amateur's passion for impromptu musicales. Jefferson, who is said to have practiced three hours daily on the cello in these student days, was assigned performing parts.

Thus early the seamless web of knowledge, the Baconian challenge to take all knowledge for his empire became Jefferson's delight. He himself reflected in later years that he had been "a hard student" and his orderly, analytical notes on Montesquieu, Shaftesbury, Locke among others—as well as his careful annotation of the history of law and his more personal selections and comments in his literary commonplace book—bear him out. But important too were the occasions for good conversation, with affable and courteous manners, and the city pleasures of theatre-going, attendance at concerts, games and convivial meetings at the Williamsburg cafe. When Jefferson came to the ultimate test of defining his basic moral values, the use of the phrase "the pursuit of happiness" encompassed all these substantial, intellectual, artistic, and friendly human associations.

Tall, red-haired, soft-spoken, and without a trace of arrogance, Jefferson traveled the path from law to public life that was even more compelling in Virginia than in Massachusetts. Henry Adams in characteristic exaggeration once propounded that "Law and politics were the only objects of Virginian thought; but within these bounds the Virginians achieved triumphs." Wythe, Jefferson, Madison, Marshall—these four alone, and at close distance dozens of others—attest to what is correct in the Adams judgment. By the time Jefferson appeared in Philadelphia, aged thirty-three, to represent Virginia at the second Continental Congress, he had practiced law, served as a member of the House of Burgesses for Albemarle County from 1769 on, and had appeared in print as the author of a distinguished essay on the oppressive course of British rule in America, and the rationale of American rights, *A Summary View of the Rights of British America,* which had placed him in the vanguard of the revolutionary leadership in his state. In the spring of 1776, when he was assigned to write the Declaration of Independence for Congress, he stepped across the threshold of "The Old Dominion" to enter the world stage as an American founder. We have John Adams' testimony that he, like the other members of the Committee on the Declaration, deferred to the younger man for this coveted role because Jefferson possessed the reputation of having written a most handsome public paper ("A Summary View") and was known to the delegates for the felicity of his pen.

In May, before Jefferson was appointed to a committee of five to prepare a Declaration, he had written urgently to political associates in Virginia asking to be recalled so that he might help to draft a new state constitution. Like John Adams, he sensed that Americans, who were about to solicit the attention of a candid world in their quest for freedom and self-government, had best create the framework of orderly republican institutions. "It is the whole object of the present controversy," he affirmed; "for should a bad government be instituted for us in future, it had been as well to have accepted at first the bad one offered to us from beyond the water without the risk of expense of contest." Through a series of accidental circumstances, Jefferson's draft of a constitution for Virginia arrived late in the proceedings of the Virginia Convention but nonetheless his preamble and several other features were incorporated into the Virginia constitution of 1776. Shortly after, Jefferson was pressed into one of the most demanding assignments that could be dealt to a legal reformer. He was put on a committee charged with the revision of Virginia's laws, and since he was Jefferson, he alone drafted 126 bills before this Herculean task was over. His aim was to bring the laws of Virginia into conformity with republican principles, creating a system "by which every fibre would be eradicated of ancient or future aristocracy; and a foundation laid for a government truly republican." Justly famous among these important bills in the revisal of 1770 was the Bill for establishing religious freedom, a bill called by Julian Boyd "Jefferson's declaration of intellectual and spiritual independence." Unlike some of his other great bills, this one was at long last enacted into law in 1786, the first piece of legislation ever to provide expressly for full religious freedom. In this contribution alone, Jefferson advanced far beyond his revered John Locke whose philosophy of toleration "stopped short," as Jefferson said, of the full freedom required by the independent intelligence and conscience of man.

Other significant bills which contributed to the fame of "the philosophical legislation of Virginia" in France and throughout Europe in the decade of the 1780s were "A Bill on the more General Diffusion of Knowledge" and the bills abolishing primogeniture and entail. The object of the diffusion of knowledge bill was to "qualify citizens to under-stand their rights, to maintain them, and to exercise with intelligence their parts in self-government." As means to this end, Jefferson pro-posed a comprehensive new plan of education for the commonwealth of Virginia, providing for free elementary schools for all future citizens, and various higher levels of free education for students of proven ability or talent. This bill must be viewed as part of the revolutionary transformation of society that Jefferson considered to be the practical outcome of the ideals professed in the Declaration. It suffered the fate shared by many later wise educational proposals in America; it could not pass the legislature on grounds of "too much expence."

It was worth notice that Jefferson was also consciously trying to effect reform in the language of the law, as well as in its content. Eager to open the laws to the hard-headed intelligence of citizens who might nevertheless be perfectly innocent of legal scholarship, he tried to get rid of the barbarisms of legal jargon, ornate, indirect, and repetitive phrasing beneath which the logic of the law was often buried. Beyond any man of his time, Jefferson had grasped the central principles that a free society flourished with the freely flowing intelligence of its citizens; and that communication, on the most extensive basis possible, was in-dispensable to governments based upon the consent of the people. Both as means and as ends, the morality of intelligence would conduct men to freedom and renew their faith.

He was in no sense a provincial Virginia planter, consequently, when he embarked for Europe in 1784 on a mission to join John Adams and Benjamin Franklin in negotiating treaties of commerce for the needy new United States. His success in Paris was second only to Franklin's, whose affectionate introduction of Jefferson to his European network of friends smoothed his path. Never did an American enter upon "the vaunted scene of Europe" with more ardor and more determination to study the best of European society, art, architecture, technology, inven-tion, agriculture—even cuisine, in order to raise the level of life and culture at home. Thus, observant travel notes were the product of one phase of Jefferson's personal conquest of the old world. But his official duties were pressing and important, especially after Franklin's return to America when Jefferson was appointed American Minister in France. Moreover, as a good friend of Lafayette and his circle, Jefferson was consulted unofficially for political advice by this group who were the leaders of the liberal "Patriot Party" in the early days of the French Revolution. In sum, the crowded years of 1784–1789 challenged Jeffer-son to compare his values and philosophy, his own country's qualities and aspirations with those of France and indeed Europe as a civilization. On the whole, they confirmed his earlier beliefs about free, re-publican government. With all the animated discussions he partook of in the most brilliant salons, and the profuse opportunities he seized for opera and theatre, he gained cosmopolitan sophistication—but nothing profoundly new in the way of ideas. Matters of emphasis changed, of course. He rethought his position on natural rights, and henceforth stressed, as he had not before, the fundamental importance of economic rights. In connection with his powerful phrase, "the earth belongs to the living," he developed his ideas of the primary claims men had upon society for the opportunity to work and find satisfaction for their economic needs. He was sensitive to human suffering and could not be indifferent to the crushing poverty of the masses of men in the cities and the peasantry in the countryside. These miseries, this inhuman indigence and accompanying ignorance he attributed to the "oppression" of stupid or self-indulgent government policy. Monarchy, which he had always condemned on grounds of self-respect and free-dom of action, he now detested as a visible system of evil that ground the faces of the poor. A new depth of moral passion awoke in him in Europe. This fact goes a long way in explaining the character of his feelings about the French Revolution. The opening events of this fate-ful upheaval he hailed as "the first chapter of the history of European liberty."

Even these few remarks about Jefferson in Paris would be inexcus-able without at least a gesture towards the more personal side of his life there. He managed to surround himself with his adored and adoring daughters, Martha and Maria; and having placed them in a fine convent school, directed their studies and reading, even the details of their dress on important occasions, in a manner sufficiently attentive to violate the canons of so-called "permissiveness" which modern society has come to tolerate. He became an intimate friend of John Adams in these years and of his splendid lady and her young ones. Across the water, Madison was Jefferson's most valued correspondent, informing him of the course and climate of political changes at home; but across the Channel, when Adams became the American Ambassa-dor at the Court of St. James's, Jefferson had an acute countryman nearby with whom he could review problems and share information and impressions. For example, as each of these diplomats received news of the new Federal Constitution, they exchanged appraising criti-cisms. Most affecting of all the events of these years, however, was the attractive middle-aged widower's infatuation with the ravishingly beautiful Mrs. Maria Cosway, portrait painter, musician, childlike lady of fashion—an exquisitely flirtatious creature of sensibility, gayety, and melancholy. Jefferson's interest in Maria kept within bounds. But she remained a bright and glowing image in his emotional life while he lived. Their correspondence, once he had resumed his high but sober tasks in the United States, dwindled through the years; yet Jefferson's last letter to her from Monticello was dated 1822, when, as he described himself to her, he had become "octogenary."

In 1789 Jefferson returned to the United States for a "visit," to find himself under pressure as soon as he put his foot on American soil to remain at home and accept the post of Secretary of State in the new government under the Constitution. After strong misgivings and considerable delay, Jefferson joined the small Cabinet family of President Washington and soon found himself at close range with Hamilton, the Secretary of the Treasury. The classic enmity between these two brilliant men began very early: in 1790, it is already apparent in the clashing opinions sent to Washington on the question of arrearages in soldiers' pay in Virginia. As the enmity developed, and led to Jefferson's resignation as Secretary of State in December of 1793 (he expressed relief at quitting "the hated occupation of politics") the dynamics of a cleavage into two major parties had been set in motion. Jefferson and Madison, as joint leaders of the opposition party, soon captured for themselves the appealing name of "Republicans"—an appeal far more extensive throughout the country than that of "Federalists." The entire decade of the 1790s, whether Jefferson was in retirement in Virginia, or at the capitol in Philadelphia, was intensely political for him in the hated sense. Fighting was rough on both sides, partly because big issues were at stake concerning the survival of democratic principles and institutions, and partly because of the dangerous inroads on the independence and growth of the infant United States by both England and France. To Jefferson and Madison as leaders of the emerging Republican Party must go the credit for creating and preserving a two-party system as a viable instrument of real political choice, and thus the *sine qua non* of free government.

In the plainer terms of political success and failure, Jefferson's Presidency commands attention. The results of a poll of the opinions of professional historians made by Arthur M. Schlesinger place Jefferson as one of the six "great" Presidents, the "Olympians" among all American statesmen. The grounds for this estimate of Jefferson were various: his successful negotiation of a turning point in the nation's history, by extending the national boundaries from the Mississippi to the Rockies; he "advanced the cause of human rights through precept and example"; he strengthened the powers of the Presidency, by his adroit management of the Congress and other means. Franklin Delano Roosevelt, himself a "great," suggested an entirely different basis for evaluating Jefferson's worth as President. He valued Jefferson as the deepest student of the cross-currents of our folk life, the hopes and fears of the common people. He praised Jefferson's "consecration" to social justice and to the freedom of the human mind. Interestingly enough, another "great," Woodrow Wilson, shifted the focus to a broader horizon still when he said "The immortality of Thomas Jefferson does not lie in any one of his achievements, but in his attitude toward mankind."

Thus, when the battles over the Kentucky and Virginia Resolutions, the constitutionality of the Bank of the United States, the Embargo policy, even Jefferson's "Agrarianism" or balanced budget fiscal policy are over, the campaign to deepen and extend Jefferson's "attitude toward mankind" is still being waged. The curious fact is that Jefferson's philosophy of human nature, and his profound understanding of the process of significant social order and social reform, made him insist that he had realized something substantial of the high ideals of " '76" and yet know that he had clearly failed to realize all he would have desired; and that successive generations of Americans would find themselves struggling with the agonizing ambiguities and tragic limitations similar to those for which he had expended a nonetheless *fulfilling* life! As he spoke across the barriers of time and space to men who would be born after he had died, he prepared instructions to his daughter that he wished only these three things inscribed on his tombstone— "because by these, as testimonials that I have lived, I wish most to be remembered:

Author of the Declaration of Independence; of the Statute of Virginia for Religious Freedom and Father of the University of Virginia."

The galaxy of his nation's highest office which he had held he passed over silently to choose the meaning of his life—his deepest and most abiding values. These were: political freedom, so that man may live with the dignity of a human person; equality, so that moral concern for every man, woman, and child may strengthen his chance to live a fulfilling life and lessen his chance of being distorted into a creature of irrational violence and hatred; religious freedom, so that man's ultimate reading of his being and of nature may be free of coercive or persuasive intrusion by the state or organized pressure groups of his fellows; and intellectual freedom or freedom of the mind, the underlying pervasive value entering into the creation and safeguarding of the other freedoms. For this "freedom of the mind" education must be available, ideally from the cradle to the grave, for all.

The University of Virginia, the "darling" project of Jefferson's old age at Monticello after his retirement from politics, represented to him the culmination of his early love of the classics, his later induction into the enlightened and liberating sciences that could be put to use to improve the human estate, his long pilgrimage of test and trial in the hard decisions and bitter conflicts of creating and serving a powerful government based on faith in the people and functioning by the mandate of their consent. The University was more than that—it was a final embodiment of his distinctive ideal of "the pursuit of happiness." What greater happiness was there than learning, the love of books, of writing, of ideas, of learning, teaching, communicating? His last years were spent fussing over library catalogues for the University, planning the curriculum, the administration. Even the buildings were grouped as an "academical village" graced with serpentine walls and well-proportioned buildings—that art might enhance the students' lives.

On July 4, 1826, fifty years to the day since his Declaration of Independence had gone forth on its immortal journey, Jefferson died. He died a poor man, in debt, his extensive land holdings reduced in value through impersonal factors beyond his control, his capital savings nonexistent because of his long absences from Monticello for the three decades of active public service. The irony of this "planter aristocrat," who freed some of his slaves in his last will but could not afford to free them all, was that he poured his soul into the vision of human rights that he bequeathed to all his countrymen.

Lest this image be tarnished today, it is important to recall, if only briefly, Jefferson's efforts toward the abolition of slavery. Despite the fact that he was a man of his time and culture, from his first entry into politics in 1769 he made an effort in the Virginia legislature "for permission of the emancipation of the slaves, which was rejected." Again, in his draft of the Declaration of Independence, he declared that the King "waged cruel war against human nature itself, violating its most sacred rights of life and liberty in the persons of a distant people who never offended him, captivating and carrying them into slavery in another hemisphere. . . . Determined to keep open a market where men should be bought and sold, he has prostituted his negative for suppressing every legislative attempt to prohibit or to restrain this execrable commerce." This clause was stricken out on the floor of Congress. Even more important was Jefferson's proposal in 1784, in his "Report of Government for the Western Territories," "that after the year 1800 of the Christian era, there should be no slavery nor involuntary servitude in any of the said states." Richard Morris, the historian, recently stated that had Congress adopted Jefferson's proposal, "slavery would have been forbidden in *all* the Western territory after 1800, not only in the Northwest as it was by the Ordinance of 1787, and the grounds for the Civil War could have been removed." Finally, Jefferson's sentiments for equality reappear in 1814 in his letter to Edward Coles, President Madison's private secretary, who later removed with his freed slaves to Illinois, and became Governor of that state, a man heroically committed to the cause of abolition. Jefferson wrote, "The love of justice and the love of country plead equally the cause of this people and it is a moral reproach to us that they should have pleaded it so long in vain, and should have produced not a single effort, nay, I fear not much serious willingness to relieve them and ourselves from our present condition of moral and political reprobation. . . . Yet the hour of emancipation is advancing, in the march of time."

It is against this setting of the American Experiment as a continuing revolution that we may view Jefferson's last extant letter, written less than two weeks before his death, regretfully declining the invitation to be present in Washington at the celebration of the fiftieth anniversary of American Independence. "All eyes are opened, or opening, to the rights of man. The general spread of the light of science has already laid open to every view the palpable truth, that the mass of mankind has not been born with saddles on their backs, nor a favored few booted and spurred, ready to ride them legitimately, by the grace of God. These are grounds of hope for others. For ourselves, let the annual return of this day forever refresh our recollections of these rights, and an undiminished devotion to them."

Perhaps the last word should be the poet's—Robert Frost musing on "the pursuit of happiness":

> *That's a hard mystery of Jefferson's.*
> *What did he mean? Of course the easy way*
> *Is to decide it simply isn't true.*
> *It may not be. I heard a fellow say so.*
> *But never mind, the Welshman got it planted*
> *Where it will trouble us a thousand years.*
> *Each age will have to reconsider it.*

Chronology of the Life of Jefferson

1743	Born April 13, Shadwell, Virginia.
1760	Attends William and Mary College until 1762.
1762	Reads law with George Wythe until 1767.
1767	Admitted to the Bar.
1769	Member, House of Burgesses until 1776.
1774	"A Summary View of the Rights of British America."
1775	Attends Continental Congress.
1776	Serves in Congress and writes the "Declaration of Independence." Attends Virginia General Assembly and serves on Commitee to revise the laws of Virginia. Drafts a Constitution for Virginia—only its preamble adopted.
1777	Elected to House of Delegates and serves until 1779.
1779	Elected Governor of Virginia for two-year term. Reports on proposed "Revisal of the Laws of Virginia," including "Bills for the General Diffusion of Knowledge" and for "Establishment of Religious Freedom."
1780	Elected to American Philosophical Society.
1782	Drafts another constitution for Virginia.
1783	Elected to Congress—drafts report on the definitive treaty of peace which was eventually adopted.
1784	Presents plan for the government of the Western Territories. Appointed to join Franklin and Adams in negotiating treaties of commerce. Arrives in Paris, August 8.
1785	Succeeds Franklin as Minister to Versailles. Publishes "Notes on the State of Virginia."
1789	Arrives home, Monticello, December for "visit." Remains in U.S. for the rest of his life.
1790	Secretary of State in new Cabinet under President Washington.
1791	Opinion of the Constitutionality of the Bank of the United States. Letter appears as Preface to Paine's "Rights of Man."

1793	Resigns as Secretary of State and retires to Monticello.
1797	Begins term as Vice-President of the U.S. Elected President of the American Philosophical Society, and serves until 1815.
1798	Organizes effort for Kentucky and Virginia Resolutions and drafts Kentucky Resolutions.
1801	Delivers first Inaugural and takes office as third President of the U.S. Only American of his period to be elected as associé étranger of the Institute of France.
1809	Leaves office and retires to Monticello.
1812	Resumes correspondence with Adams.
1826	Dies at Monticello, Virginia, on July 4, a few hours before John Adams.

JEFFERSON LOOKS AT THE WORLD

1

Jefferson's "original Rough draught" of the Declaration of Independence

In a last-minute effort to dissuade the delegates of the Continental Congress from voting acceptance of the Declaration of Independence, John Dickinson urged them not to "brace the Storm in a Skiff made of Paper." Never in human history has a skiff of paper carried so many brave men safely to port. As it turned out, the Declaration accomplished the very objectives which Dickinson enumerated as unrealistic. It did "animate the People," "convince foreign Powers of our Strength and Unanimity," and even secure their "aid in consequence thereof." Equally important, it began the irreversible process of binding together the previously separate colonies into a union, linking the political independence of the United States with a government distinctively and pervasively based upon the freely given consent of the people.

As for the long-range influence of the Delcaration of Independence, one can trace clues of its inexhaustible hold upon the American mind throughout the entire spread of our history. But the worldwide impact of the philosophy of human rights which Jefferson formulated in the Declaration fulfills another dimension of the author's democratic faith. We must go to the enemy camp, to Henry Adams whose savor for flogging Jefferson never lost its edge, for the statement that "Jefferson aspired beyond the ambition of a nationality, and embraced in his view the whole future of man." The influence of the Declaration can be seen subsequently not only in the French Declaration of the Rights of Man but in other parts of Europe and South America and in our own time in the United Nations, as well as in new-modeled states in Africa and Asia. For these and other reasons, Jefferson's "sublime document" is widely considered to be "the most timeless and eloquent of all American historical papers."

The text printed below is Jefferson's so-called "original Rough draught." [1] *In fact, there were two earlier drafts (see Boyd, Vol. I, 413–33). One fragmentary draft detailed sixteen charges against the Crown, and served as the opening section of Jefferson's plan of a Constitution for Virginia. However, the so-called "original Rough draught" is the most complete and purely Jeffersonian version of the Declaration. The text given below includes the few minor changes made by John Adams and Benjamin Franklin, before the Committee of Five was ready to submit the document to Congress. What emerged from Congress, after it had altered and made several substantial deletions in Jefferson's composition, is the final text whose phraseology is familiar to all Americans.*

In the opinion of many commentators, Congress improved upon Jefferson's text. Jefferson himself, then aged 33, and the youngest man on the illustrious Committee of Five (composed of Franklin, Adams, Sherman, and Robert R. Livingston as well as Jefferson) was understandably distressed with the many Congressional cooks who he felt, were spoiling his broth. He was especially angered by the deletion of his clause "reprobating the enslaving the inhabitants of Africa," and charged that it was "struck out in complaisance to South Carolina & Georgia, who had never attempted to restrain the importation of slaves, and who on the contrary still wished to continue it." He added: "Our Northern brethren also I believe felt a little tender under these censures; for tho' their people have very few slaves themselves yet they had been pretty considerable carriers of them to others."

A DECLARATION OF THE REPRESENTATIVES OF THE UNITED STATES OF AMERICA, IN GENERAL CONGRESS ASSEMBLED

When in the course of human events it becomes necessary for a people to advance from that subordination in which they have hith-

---

[1] From *The Papers of Thomas Jefferson,* Julian Boyd, ed. (Princeton, N.J.: Princeton University Press, 1950), I, 423–27. (Hereafter referred to as Boyd.) Selections from Boyd are reprinted by permission of the publisher.

erto remained, & to assume among the powers of the earth the equal
& independant station to which the laws of nature & of nature's god
entitle them, a decent respect to the opinions of mankind requires
that they should declare the causes which impel them to the change.

We hold these truths to be sacred & undeniable, that all men are
created equal & independant, that from that equal creation they derive
rights inherent & inalienable, among which are the preservation of life,
& liberty, & the pursuit of happiness; that to secure these ends, governments are instituted among men, deriving their just powers from
the consent of the governed; that whenever any form of government
shall become destructive of these ends, it is the right of the people to
alter or to abolish it, & to institute new government, laying it's foundation on such principles & organising it's powers in such form, as to
them shall seem most likely to effect their safety & happiness. prudence
indeed will dictate that governments long established should not be
changed for light & transient causes: and accordingly all experience
hath shewn that mankind are more disposed to suffer while evils are
sufferable, than to right themselves by abolishing the forms to which
they are accustomed. but when a long train of abuses & usurpations,
begun at a distinguished period, & pursuing invariably the same object, evinces a design to subject them to arbitrary power, it is their
right, it is their duty, to throw off such government & to provide new
guards for their future security. such has been the patient sufferance of
these colonies; & such is now the necessity which constrains them to
expunge their former systems of government. the history of his present
majesty, is a history of unremitting injuries and usurpations, among
which no one fact stands single or solitary to contradict the uniform
tenor of the rest, all of which have in direct object the establishment
of an absolute tyranny over these states. to prove this, let facts be submitted to a candid world, for the truth of which we pledge a faith yet
unsullied by falsehood.

he has refused his assent to laws the most wholesome and necessary
  for the public good:
he has forbidden his governors to pass laws of immediate & pressing
  importance, unless suspended in their operation till his assent
  should be obtained; and when so suspended, he has neglected utterly
  to attend to them.
he has refused to pass other laws for the accomodation of large dis-
  tricts of people unless those people would relinquish the right of
  representation, a right inestimable to them, & formidable to tyrants
  alone:

he has dissolved Representative houses repeatedly & continually, for opposing with manly firmness his invasions on the rights of the people:

he has refused for a long space of time to cause others to be elected, whereby the legislative powers, incapable of annihilation, have returned to the people at large for their exercise, the state remaining in the mean time exposed to all the dangers of invasion from without, & convulsions within:

he has endeavored to prevent the population of these states; for that purpose obstructing the laws for naturalization of foreigners. refusing to pass others to encourage their migrations hither; & raising the conditions of new appropriations of lands:

he has suffered the administration of justice totally to cease in some of these colonies, refusing his assent to laws for estblishing judiciary powers:

he has made our judges dependant on his will alone, for the tenure of their offices, and amount of their salaries:

he has erected a multitude of new offices by a self-assumed power, & sent hither swarms of officers to harrass our people & eat out their substance:

he has kept among us in times of peace standing armies & ships of war:

he has affected to render the military, independant of & superior to the civil power:

he has combined with others to subject us to a jurisdiction foreign to our constitutions and unacknoleged by our laws; giving his assent to their pretended acts of legislation, for quartering large bodies of armed troops among us;

> for protecting them by a mock-trial from punishment for any murders they should commit on the inhabitants of these states;
> for cutting off our trade with all parts of the world;
> for imposing taxes on us without our consent;
> for depriving us of the benefits of trial by jury;
> for transporting us beyond seas to be tried for pretended offences:
> for taking away our charters, & altering fundamentally the forms of our governments;
> for suspending our own legislatures & declaring themselves invested with power to legislate for us in all cases whatsoever:

he has abdicated government here, withdrawing his governors, & declaring us out of his allegiance & protection:

he has plundered our seas, ravaged our coasts, burnt our towns & destroyed the lives of our people:

he is at this time transporting large armies of foreign mercenaries to compleat the works of death, desolation & tyranny, already begun with circumstances of cruelty & perfidy unworthy the head of a civilized nation:

he has endeavored to bring on the inhabitants of our frontiers the merciless Indian savages, whose known rule of warfare is an undistinguished destruction of all ages, sexes, & conditions of existence:

he has incited treasonable insurrections in our fellow-subjects, with the allurements of forfeiture & confiscation of our property:

he has waged cruel war against human nature itself, violating it's most sacred rights of life & liberty in the persons of a distant people who never offended him, captivating & carrying them into slavery in another hemisphere, or to incur miserable death in their transportation thither. this piratical warfare, the opprobrium of *infidel* powers, is the warfare of the CHRISTIAN king of Great Britain. determined to keep open a market where MEN should be bought & sold, he has prostituted his negative for supressing every legislative attempt to prohibit or to restrain this execrable commerce: and that this assemblage of horrors might want no fact of distinguished die, he is now exciting those very people to rise in arms among us, and to purchase that liberty of which *he* has deprived them, by murdering the people upon whom *he* also obtruded them; thus paying off former crimes committed against the *liberties* of one people, with crimes which he urges them to commit against the *lives* of another.

in every stage of these oppressions we have petitioned for redress in the most humble terms; our repeated petitions have been answered by repeated injury. a prince whose character is thus marked by every act which may define a tyrant, is unfit to be the ruler of a people who mean to be free. future ages will scarce believe that the hardiness of one man, adventured within the short compass of 12 years only, on so many acts of tyranny without a mask, over a people fostered & fixed in principles of liberty.

Nor have we been wanting in attentions to our British brethren. we have warned them from time to time of attempts by their legislature to extend a jurisdiction over these our states. we have reminded them of the circumstances of our emigration & settlement here, no one of which could warrant so strange a pretension: that these were effected at the expence of our own blood & treasure, unassisted by the wealth or the strength of Great Britain: that in constituting indeed our several forms of government, we had adopted one common king, thereby laying a foundation for perpetual league & amity with them:

but that submission to their parliament was no part of our constitution, nor ever in idea, if history may be credited: and we appealed to their native justice & magnanimity, as well as to the ties of our common kindred to disavow these usurpations which were likely to interrupt our correspondence & connection. they too have been deaf to the voice of justice & of consanguinity, & when occasions have been given them, by the regular course of their laws, of removing from their councils the disturbers of our harmony, they have by their free election re-established them in power. at this very time too they are permitting their chief magistrate to send over not only soldiers of our common blood, but Scotch & foreign mercenaries to invade & deluge us in blood. these facts have given the last stab to agonizing affection, and manly spirit bids us to renounce for ever these unfeeling brethren. we must endeavor to forget our former love for them, and to hold them as we hold the rest of mankind, enemies in war, in peace friends. we might have been a free & a great people together; but a communication of grandeur & of freedom it seems is below their dignity. be it so, since they will have it: the road to glory & happiness is open to us too; we will climb it in a separate state, and acquiesce in the necessity which pronounces our everlasting Adieu!

We therefore the representatives of the United States of America in General Congress assembled do, in the name & by authority of the good people of these states, reject and renounce all allegiance & subjection to the kings of Great Britain & all others who may hereafter claim by, through, or under them; we utterly dissolve & break off all political connection which may have heretofore subsisted between us & the people or parliament of Great Britain; and finally we do assert and declare these colonies to be free and independant states, and that as free & independant states they shall hereafter have power to levy war, conclude peace, contract alliances, establish commerce, & to do all other acts and things which independant states may of right do. And for the support of this declaration we mutually pledge to each other our lives, our fortunes, & our sacred honour.

2
The Revisal of the Laws, 1776–1786

In the autumn of 1776, Jefferson wrote a bill calling for a revision of the laws of Virginia, and like many another good man with bold ideas was at once put on the committee charged with doing the work. The composition of this important committee is noteworthy, for the best legal minds of the Old Dominion—Edmund Pendleton, George Wythe, George Mason, and Thomas Ludwell Lee—were to be Jefferson's colleagues. But Jefferson was not only the Chairman of the Committee: he was the leading figure of the work of revisal, himself the draftsman of one hundred and twenty-six bills of the revised code. The bills Jefferson drafted were intended to bring the laws into conformity with republican principles, to create a system "by which every fibre would be eradicated of ancient or future aristocracy; and a foundation laid for a government truly republican."

Perhaps the two most important bills were the Bill for the more general diffusion of knowledge, and the Bill for establishing religious freedom. Jefferson's proposal for a comprehensive new plan of education for Virginia attempted to provide the means by which the ideals of the Declaration could trasnform the existing society. Jefferson hoped to "qualify citizens to understand their rights, to maintain them, and to exercise with intelligence their parts in self-government." The "Bill for Establishing Religious Freedom" was the indispensable accompaniment of the one for the diffusion of knowledge. Boyd has termed Jefferson's bill for religious freedom a "timeless declaration of intellectual freedom." It became, when enacted into law under Madison's guidance in 1785, the first piece of legislation in history to provide the thorough separation of church and state on a basis of man's natural right to full freedom of thought and conscience.

PREAMBLE FROM A BILL FOR THE MORE GENERAL DIFFUSION OF KNOWLEDGE [1]

Whereas it appeareth that however certain forms of government are better calculated than others to protect individuals in the free exercise of their natural rights, and are at the same time themselves better guarded against degeneracy, yet experience hath shewn, that even under the best forms, those entrusted with power have, in time, and by slow operations, perverted it into tyranny; and it is believed that the most effectual means of preventing this would be, to illuminate, as far as practicable, the minds of the people at large, and more especially to give them knowledge of those facts, which history exhibiteth, that, possessed thereby of the experience of other ages and countries, they may be enabled to know ambition under all its shapes, and prompt to exert their natural powers to defeat its purposes; And whereas it is generally true that that people will be happiest whose laws are best, and are best administered, and that laws will be wisely formed, and honestly administered, in proportion as those who form and administer them are wise and honest; whence it becomes expedient for promoting the publick happiness that those persons, whom nature hath endowed with genius and virtue, should be rendered by liberal education worthy to receive, and able to guard the sacred deposit of the rights and liberties of their fellow citizens, and that they should be called to that charge without regard to wealth, birth or other accidental condition or circumstance; but the indigence of the greater number disabling them from so educating, at their own expence, those of their children whom nature hath fitly formed and disposed to become useful instruments for the public, it is better that such should be sought for and educated at the common expence of all, than that the happiness of all should be confided to the weak or wicked:

AN ACT FOR ESTABLISHING RELIGIOUS FREEDOM (1779), PASSED IN THE ASSEMBLY OF VIRGINIA IN THE BEGINNING OF THE YEAR 1786 [2]

Well aware that Almighty God hath created the mind free; that all attempts to influence it by temporal punishments or burdens, or by

---

[1] Boyd, II, 526–27.

[2] From *The Writings of Thomas Jefferson*, Andrew A. Lipscomb and Albert Bergh, eds. (Washington, D.C.: The Thomas Jefferson Memorial Association, 1905), II, 300–303. (Hereafter referred to as Memorial Edition.)

civil incapacitations, tend only to beget habits of hypocrisy and mean-
ness, and are a departure from the plan of the Holy Author of our
religion, who being Lord both of body and mind, yet chose not to
propagate it by coercions on either, as was in his Almighty power to
do; that the impious presumption of legislators and rulers, civil as
well as ecclesiastical, who, being themselves but fallible and uninspired
men have assumed dominion over the faith of others, setting up their
own opinions and modes of thinking as the only true and infallible,
and as such endeavoring to impose them on others, hath established
and maintained false religions over the greatest part of the world,
and through all time; that to compel a man to furnish contributions
of money for the propagation of opinions which he disbelieves, is sin-
ful and tyrannical; that even the forcing him to support this or that
teacher of his own religious persuasion, is depriving him of the comfortable liberty of giving his contributions to the particular pastor
whose morals he would make his pattern, and whose powers he feels
most persuasive to righteousness, and is withdrawing from the ministry
those temporal rewards, which proceeding from an approbation of
their personal conduct, are an additional incitement to earnest and
unremitting labors for the instruction of mankind; that our civil
rights have no dependence on our religious opinions, more than our
opinions in physics or geometry; that, therefore, the proscribing any
citizen as unworthy the public confidence by laying upon him an incapacity of being called to the offices of trust and emolument, unless
he profess or renounce this or that religious opinion, is depriving him
injuriously of those privileges and advantages to which in common
with his fellow citizens he has a natural right; that it tends also to
corrupt the principles of that very religion it is meant to encourage,
by bribing, with a monopoly of worldly honors and emoluments, those
who will externally profess and conform to it; that though indeed
these are criminal who do not withstand such temptation, yet neither
are those innocent who lay the bait in their way; that to suffer the civil
magistrate to intrude his powers into the field of opinion and to restrain the profession or propagation of principles, on the supposition
of their ill tendency, is a dangerous fallacy, which at once destroys
all religious liberty, because he being of course judge of that tendency,
will make his opinions the rule of judgment, and approve or condemn
the sentiments of others only as they shall square with or differ from
his own; that it is time enough for the rightful purposes of civil government, for its offices to interfere when principles break out into
overt acts against peace and good order; and finally, that truth is
great and will prevail if left to herself, that she is the proper and

sufficient antagonist to error, and has nothing to fear from the conflict, unless by human interposition disarmed of her natural weapons, free argument and debate, errors ceasing to be dangerous when it is permitted freely to contradict them.

Be it therefore enacted by the General Assembly, That no man shall be compelled to frequent or support any religious worship, place or ministry whatsoever, nor shall be enforced, restrained, molested, or burthened in his body or goods, nor shall otherwise suffer on account of his religious opinions or belief; but that all men shall be free to profess, and by argument to maintain, their opinions in matters of religion, and that the same shall in nowise diminish, enlarge, or affect their civil capacities.

And though we well know this Assembly, elected by the people for the ordinary purposes of legislation only, have no power to restrain the acts of succeeding assemblies, constituted with the powers equal to our own, and that therefore to declare this act irrevocable, would be of no effect in law, yet we are free to declare, and do declare, that the rights hereby asserted are of the natural rights of mankind, and that if any act shall be hereafter passed to repeal the present or to narrow its operation, such act will be an infringement of natural right.

3
Notes on the State of Virginia

In the eighty-three years of Jefferson's supremely productive life, Notes on the State of Virginia *is the only full-length
book that he wrote and published. It was stimulated by the request of the Secretary of the French legation at Philadelphia,
who sought information about each of the American states from
its leading men. There were various more or less routine replies
to the questions submitted by Secretary François Marbois.
Only Jefferson's "reply" burgeoned into a book, and one that
epitomized the characteristic moral and political thought of the
American Enlightenment. Partly because of the nature of the
queries put to him, but also because Jefferson typically preferred
the close conjunction of facts and theories, his* Notes *are both a
mine of information about Virginia, which was at the time the
largest state in the union, claiming territory that embraced a
third of the North American continent, and a compendium of
his philosophy of experimental naturalism. The book is suffused
with his sense of the physical and moral character of his native
land, and may justly be considered the first memorable defence
of the budding genius of American culture.*

Written in 1780–81, the Notes *were carried by their author to
Paris in 1784 where he permitted them to be privately printed
in an edition of two hundred copies in 1785. The decision for a
private printing remains something of a mystery to this day. In
part, it reflected Jefferson's schooled sense of propriety. He was
a diplomatic representative of the revolutionary government of
the United States and preferred to avoid the light of publicity on
views that were after all his own personal judgments of persons,
places, and ideas. Initially, he also seems to have regarded as
potentially explosive his critical remarks about the Virginia constitution and politics and his unqualified condemnation of slavery
as an evil institution that corrupted masters and slaves alike. His
candid discussion of religious freedom, including his pithy
defence of the right to* disbelieve *("It does me no harm if my
neighbor says there are twenty gods or no god. It neither picks my*

pocket nor breaks my leg.") was sure to involve him in clerical attacks and the kind of religious inquest which he loathed as a violation of personal privacy. In any event, the book could not be kept a private or semi-private affair. It soon appeared in a "bad French translation," and subsequently in an authorized edition published by Stockdale, the London bookseller. English and European reviewers, and American friends and enemies who discussed it with much excitement, ensured it a considerable degree of reknown. Even its statistical surveys and charts could not dampen the author's vivacious style nor the interest of his original thought on representative democracy, his criticism of European scientific theories, and his fresh theories of the role of education, architecture, and art in a free modern society. Despite the modesty with which Jefferson habitually said he only "succeeded" to Franklin's place as American Minister to France, but could "never replace him," the Notes clearly established him as a persona grata in the liberal and free-thinking circles of Paris, the central capital of Europe in the 1780s.

ON THE LAW "TO DIFFUSE KNOWLEDGE MORE GENERALLY THROUGH THE MASS OF THE PEOPLE" [1]

. . . The general objects of this law are to provide an education adapted to the years, to the capacity, and the condition of every one, and directed to their freedom and happiness. Specific details were not proper for the law. These must be the business of the visitors entrusted with its execution. The first stage of this education being the schools of the hundreds, wherein the great mass of the people will receive their instruction, the principal foundations of future order will be laid here. Instead therefore of putting the Bible and Testament into the hands of the children, at an age when their judgments are not sufficiently matured for religious enquiries, their memories may here be stored with the most useful facts from Grecian, Roman, European and American history. The first elements of morality too may be instilled into their minds; such as, when further developed as their judgments advance in strength, may teach them how to work out their own greatest happiness, by shewing them that it does not depend on the condition of life in which chance has placed them, but is always the result of a good conscience, good health, occupation, and freedom

[1] From *Notes on the State of Virginia*, William Peden, ed. (Chapel Hill: University of North Carolina Press, 1955), pp. 147–49. Reprinted by permission of the publisher and the Institute of Early American History and Culture.

in all just pursuits.—Those whom either the wealth of their parents or the adoption of the state shall destine to higher degrees of learning, will go on to the grammar schools, which constitute the next stage, there to be instructed in the languages. . . . —As soon as they are of sufficient age, it is supposed they will be sent on from the grammar schools to the university, which constitutes our third and last stage, there to study those sciences which may be adapted to their views.— By that part of our plan which prescribes the selection of the youths of genius from among the classes of the poor, we hope to avail the state of those talents which nature has sown as liberally among the poor as the rich, but which perish without use, if not sought for and cultivated. But of all the views of this law none is more important, none more legitimate, than that of rendering the people the safe, as they are the ultimate, guardians of their own liberty. For this purpose the reading in the first stage, where *they* will receive their whole education, is proposed, as has been said, to be chiefly historical. History by apprising them of the past will enable them to judge of the future; it will avail them of the experience of other times and other nations; it will qualify them as judges of the actions and designs of men; it will enable them to know ambition under every disguise it may assume; and knowing it, to defeat its views. In every government on earth is some trace of human weakness, some germ of corruption and degeneracy, which cunning will discover, and wickedness insensibly open, cultivate, and improve. Every government degenerates when trusted to the rulers of the people alone. The people themselves therefore are its only safe depositories. And to render even them safe their minds must be improved to a certain degree. This indeed is not all that is necessary, though it be essentially necessary. An amendment of our constitution must here come in aid of the public education. The influence over government must be shared among all the people. If every individual which composes their mass participates of the ultimate authority, the government will be safe; because the corrupting the whole mass will exceed any private resources of wealth: and public ones cannot be provided but by levies on the people. In this case every man would have to pay his own price. The government of Great-Britain has been corrupted, because but one man in ten has a right to vote for members of parliament. The sellers of the government therefore get nine-tenths of their price clear. It has been thought that corruption is restrained by confining the right of suffrage to a few of the wealthier of the people: but it would be more effectually restrained by an extension of that right to such numbers as would bid defiance to the means of corruption.

ON THE FREEDOM OF RELIGION [2]

. . . The error seems not sufficiently eradicated, that the operations of the mind, as well as the acts of the body, are subject to the coercion of the laws. But our rulers can have authority over such natural rights only as we have submitted to them The rights of conscience we never submitted, we could not submit. We are answerable for them to our God. The legitimate powers of government extend to such acts only as are injurious to others. But it does me no injury for my neighbour to say there are twenty gods, or no god. It neither picks my pocket nor breaks my leg. If it be said, his testimony in a court of justice cannot be relied on, reject it then, and be the stigma on him. Constraint may make him worse by making him a hypocrite, but it will never make him a truer man. It may fix him obstinately in his errors, but will not cure them. Reason and free enquiry are the only effectual agents against error. Give a loose to them, they will support the true religion, by bringing every false one to their tribunal, to the test of their investigation. They are the natural enemies of error, and of error only. Had not the Roman government permitted free enquiry, Christianity could never have been introduced. Had not free enquiry been indulged, at the æra of the reformation, the corruptions of Christianity could not have been purged away. If it be restrained now, the present corruptions will be protected, and new ones encouraged. Was the government to prescribe to us our medicine and diet, our bodies would be in such keeping as our souls are now. Thus in France the emetic was once forbidden as a medicine, and the potatoe as an article of food. Government is just as infallible too when it fixes systems in physics. Galileo was sent to the inquisition for affirming that the earth was a sphere: the government had declared it to be as flat as a trencher, and Galileo was obliged to abjure his error. This error however at length prevailed, the earth became a globe, and Descartes declared it was whirled round its axis by a vortex. The government in which he lived was wise enough to see that this was no question of civil jurisdiction, or we should all have been involved by authority in vortices. In fact, the vortices have been exploded, and the Newtonian principle of gravitation is now more firmly established, on the basis of reason, than it would be were the government to step in, and to make it an article of necessary faith. Reason and experiment have been indulged, and error has fled before them. It is error alone

[2] *Notes*, ibid, pp. 159–60.

which needs the support of government. Truth can stand by itself. Subject opinion to coercion: whom will you make your inquisitors? Fallible men; men governed by bad passions, by private as well as public reasons. And why subject it to coercion? To produce uniformity. But is uniformity of opinion desirable? No more than of face and stature. Introduce the bed of Procrustes then, and as there is danger that the large men may beat the small, make us all of a size, by lopping the former and stretching the latter. Difference of opinion is advantageous in religion. The several sects perform the office of a Censor morum over each other. Is uniformity attainable? Millions of innocent men, women, and children, since the introduction of Christianity, have been burnt, tortured, fined, imprisoned; yet we have not advanced one inch towards uniformity. What has been the effect of coercion? To make one half the world fools, and the other half hypocrites. To support roguery and error all over the earth. Let us reflect that it is inhabited by a thousand millions of people. That these profess probably a thousand different systems of religion. That ours is but one of that thousand. That if there be but one right, and ours that one, we should wish to see the 999 wandering sects gathered into the fold of truth. But against such a majority we cannot effect this by force. Reason and persuasion are the only practicable instruments. To make way for these, free enquiry must be indulged; and how can we wish others to indulge it while we refuse it ourselves. . . .

ON SLAVERY [3]

. . . There must doubtless be an unhappy influence on the manners of our people produced by the existence of slavery among us. The whole commerce between master and slave is a perpetual exercise of the most boisterous passions, the most unremitting despotism on the one part, and degrading submissions on the other. Our children see this, and learn to imitate it; for man is an imitative animal. This quality is the germ of all education in him. From his cradle to his grave he is learning to do what he sees others do. If a parent could find no motive either in his philanthropy or his self-love, for restraining the intemperance of passion towards his slave, it should always be a sufficient one that his child is present. But generally it is not sufficient. The parent storms, the child looks on, catches the lineaments of wrath, puts on the same airs in the circle of smaller slaves, gives a loose to his worst of passions, and thus nursed, educated, and daily exercised in

[3] *Notes,* ibid, pp. 162–63.

tyranny, cannot but be stamped by it with odious peculiarities. The man must be a prodigy who can retain his manners and morals undepraved by such circumstances. And with what execration should the statesman be loaded, who permitting one half the citizens thus to trample on the rights of the other, transforms those into despots, and these into enemies, destroys the morals of the one part, and the amor patriæ of the other. For if a slave can have a country in this world, it must be any other in preference to that in which he is born to live and labour for another: in which he must lock up the faculties of his nature, contribute as far as depends on his individual endeavours to the evanishment of the human race, or entail his own miserable condition on the endless generations proceeding from him. With the morals of the people, their industry also is destroyed. For in a warm climate, no man will labour for himself who can make another labour for him. This is so true, that of the proprietors of slaves a very small proportion indeed are ever seen to labour. And can the liberties of a nation be thought secure when we have removed their only firm basis, a conviction in the minds of the people that these liberties are of the gift of God? That they are not to be violated but with his wrath? Indeed I tremble for my country when I reflect that God is just: that his justice cannot sleep for ever: that considering numbers, nature and natural means only, a revolution of the wheel of fortune, an exchange of situation, is among possible events: that it may become probable by supernatural interference! The Almighty has no attribute which can take side with us in such a contest.—But it is impossible to be temperate and to pursue this subject through the various considerations of policy, of morals, of history natural and civil. We must be contented to hope they will force their way into every one's mind. I think a change already perceptible, since the origin of the present revolution. The spirit of the master is abating, that of the slave rising from the dust, his condition mollifying, the way I hope preparing, under the auspices of heaven, for a total emancipation, and that this is disposed, in the order of events, to be with the consent of the masters, rather than by their extirpation.

ON MANUFACTURES [4]

The political œconomists of Europe have established it as a principle that every state should endeavour to manufacture for itself: and this principle, like many others, we transfer to America, without

[4] *Notes,* ibid, pp. 164–65.

calculating the difference of circumstance which should often produce a difference of result. In Europe the lands are either cultivated, or locked up against the cultivator. Manufacture must therefore be resorted to of necessity not of choice, to support the surplus of their people. But we have an immensity of land courting the industry of the husbandman. Is it best then that all our citizens should be employed in its improvement, or that one half should be called off from that to exercise manufactures and handicraft arts for the other? Those who labour in the earth are the chosen people of God, if ever he had a chosen people, whose breasts he has made his peculiar deposit for substantial and genuine virtue. It is the focus in which he keeps alive that sacred fire, which otherwise might escape from the face of the earth. Corruption of morals in the mass of cultivators is a phænomenon of which no age nor nation has furnished an example. It is the mark set on those, who not looking up to heaven, to their own soil and industry, as does the husbandman, for their subsistance, depend for it on the casualties and caprice of customers. Dependance begets subservience and venality, suffocates the germ of virtue, and prepares fit tools for the designs of ambition. This, the natural progress and consequence of the arts, has sometimes perhaps been retarded by accidental circumstances: but, generally speaking, the proportion which the aggregate of the other classes of citizens bears in any state to that of its husbandmen, is the proportion of its unsound to its healthy parts, and is a good-enough barometer whereby to measure its degree of corruption. While we have land to labour then, let us never wish to see our citizens occupied at a work-bench, or twirling a distaff. Carpenters, masons, smiths, are wanting in husbandry: but, for the general operations of manufacture, let our work-shops remain in Europe. It is better to carry provisions and materials to workmen there, than bring them to the provisions and materials, and with them their manners and principles. The loss by the transportation of commodities across the Atlantic will be made up in happiness and permanence of government. The mobs of great cities add just so much to the support of pure government, as sores do to the strength of the human body. It is the manners and spirit of a people which perserve a republic in vigour. A degeneracy in these is a canker which soon eats to the heart of its laws and constitution.

4

The Vaunted Scene of Europe

Early in May, 1784, Congress appointed Jefferson Minister Plenipotentiary to collaborate with Franklin and Adams in securing favorable commercial treaties for the United States. Jefferson arrived in France in August, promptly fell in love with the countryside and with Paris, and willingly entered upon the demanding and multifaceted tasks of representing the interests of his struggling young country. His official duties included the preservation of America's flattering reputation for revolutionary courage and for its great new experiment in republican government. Thus, his personal tastes for consorting with the intelligentsia blended nicely with his official role, and Jefferson, the Virginian, and the American patriot leader, was soon the center of an admiring circle of savants. He always felt indebted for his easy entry into the brilliant salons of the philosophes to his older colleague, the wise and subtle Benjamin Franklin, who had been positively worshipped as an idol by the bright lights of the Enlightenment in France. When Franklin returned to the United States, and Jefferson succeeded him as Minister to France, he did his share to keep the fame of his inventive and Socratic countryman lustrous as ever.

Jefferson's five years of service as an American diplomat permitted him to travel extensively throughout Europe and included a notable visit to his friendly colleague John Adams, who was at the time serving as the first American Minister to the Court of St. James in London. Jefferson profited from both his work and his meticulously observant travels. He matured in skill and knowledge of the field of foreign governmental and trade affairs. On the other hand, Jefferson's painful encounter with the nearly beggared peasantry of France made an indelible impression upon his mind and feelings. He could never subdue this impression, no matter how much he participated busily and happily in the stimulating world of the philosophes, the liberal nobility, and the cultivated bankers and merchants who resided in or visited Paris, the most sophisticated capital of all Europe. He thus devel-

oped an ambivalence about France—he was at once attached to it as his "adopted country" and morally rejected its oppressive government and society. In effect, he found in France (and other parts of Europe) fresh confirmation of his earlier beliefs in human rights and equality, a renewed faith in "the holy cause of liberty" for which the American people had so recently sacrificed lives, property, and the relaxations of peacetime.

Jefferson hailed the coming of the French Revolution. Arm in arm with the Scottish philosopher, Dugald Stewart, he watched the opening scenes of the people's uprising with intense excitement, seeing what he termed "the opening chapter" in the history of European liberty. He helped Lafayette and his friends, the "Patriot party," to take a decided stand in favor of popular rights and representation; but in view of the lack of preparation he detected in the French people for full self-government, he urged the value of a half-way house, a liberal constitutional monarchy. Later as the Revolution took its dreadful toll in human lives, executed the King, unleashed "the terror" upon one faction of leaders after another, Jefferson continued to hope for some fruitful advance in freedom from the carnage; but privately, he was undoubtedly shaken by its destructive course, so unlike the American Revolution itself.

From the western side of the Atlantic, his mail brought news of the troubles his own country faced under the inadequate powers of the Confederation. Correspondence with his good friend, James Madison, provided a searching discussion of the basic features of the proposed new Federal Constitution.

On the point of returning home for a visit—a visit which turned into a permanent return when he found himself drafted for Washington's Cabinet as the first Secretary of State—Jefferson wrote Madison a famous letter advocating the thesis that "the earth belongs to the living." This letter may have been written with an eye to the oppressive taxation policy of Louis XVI, and a a warning voice reminding short-sighted rulers that militaristic ventures and sharp divisions between a luxuried aristocracy and an impoverished people could not and should not be sustained. But it could also apply as a general principle to all governments, including representative democracies, to teach the lesson that each generation of human beings should have the right to wrest from the earth at least a subsistence living. "Freedom from want" is perhaps the familiar modern way to phrase this basic demand.

MISSION TO EUROPE AND THE ETHICS OF PUBLIC TRUST[1]

To Abner Nash

Philadelphia Mar. 11, 1783

Dear Sir

Since I had the pleasure of seeing you at Baltimore I have further reflected on the proposition you were so kind as to make me there of entering into a partnership for the purpose of purchasing some of the escheated territory in your state. I consider it as one of those fair opportunities of bettering my situation which in private prudence I ought to adopt, and which were I to consider myself merely as a private man I should adopt without condition or hesitation. But I find it is the opinion of some gentlemen that the interests of land companies may by possibility be brought on the carpet of negotiation in Europe. Whether I may or may not participate in those negotiations remains still as incertain as it was in the moment of our conversation on this subject. However I having hitherto while concerned in the direction of public affairs made it a rule to avoid engaging in any of those enterprizes which on becoming the subjects of public deliberation might lay my judgment under bias or oblige me for fear of that to withdraw from the decision altogether, I would wish still to pursue that line of conduct. Indeed I feel the obligation to do it the stronger in proportion to the magnitude of the trust at present confided to me. If my mission to Europe be still pursued I would chuse for my own satisfaction as well as for that of Congress to have not a single interest which in any point of the negotiation might separate me from the great bulk of my countrymen, or expose me to a suspicion of having any object to pursue which might lead me astray from the general. You will therefore be sensible that my situation does not leave me an equal liberty with the other gentlemen of availing myself of this opportunity of repairing some of my losses; on the contrary that it calls for this in addition to the sacrifices I have already made. . . .

[1] Boyd, VI, 255.

EVILS OF CONFEDERATION [2]

To Richard Price

Paris, Feb. 1, 1785

Sir

The copy of your Observations on the American Revolution which you were so kind as to direct to me came duly to hand, and I should sooner have acknowledged the receipt of it but that I awaited a private conveiance for my letter, having experienced much delay and uncertainty in the posts between this place and London. I have read it with very great pleasure, as have done many others to whom I have communicated it. The spirit which it breathes is as affectionate as the observations themselves are wise and just. I have no doubt it will be reprinted in America and produce much good there. The want of power in the federal head was early perceived, and foreseen to be the flaw in our constitution which might endanger its destruction. I have the pleasure to inform you that when I left America in July the people were becoming universally sensible of this, and a spirit to enlarge the powers of Congress was becoming general. Letters and other information recently received shew that this has continued to increase, and that they are likely to remedy this evil effectually. The happiness of governments like ours, wherein the people are truly the mainspring, is that they are never to be despaired of. When an evil becomes so glaring as to strike them generally, they arrouse themselves, and it is redressed. He only is then the popular man and can get into office who shews the best dispositions to reform the evil. This truth was obvious on several occasions during the late war, and this character in our governments saved us. Calamity was our best physician. Since the peace it was observed that some nations of Europe, counting on the weakness of Congress and the little probability of a union in measure among the States, were proposing to grasp at unequal advantages in our commerce. The people are become sensible of this, and you may be assured that this evil will be immediately redressed, and redressed radically. I doubt still whether in this moment they will enlarge those powers in Congress which are necessary to keep the peace among the States. I think it possible that this may be suffered to lie till some two States commit hostilities on each other, but in that moment the hand of the union will be lifted up and interposed, and the people will themselves demand a

[2] Boyd, VII, 630–31.

general concession to Congress of means to prevent similar mischiefs. Our motto is truly "nil desperandum." The apprehensions you express of danger from the want of powers in Congress, led me to note to you this character in our governments, which, since the retreat behind the Delaware, and the capture of Charlestown, has kept my mind in perfect quiet as to the ultimate fate of our union; and I am sure, from the spirit which breathes thro your book, that whatever promises permanence to that will be a comfort to your mind. . . .

"ONE NATION ONLY" [3]

To James Madison

Paris Feb. 8, 1786

. . . I have heard with great pleasure that our assembly have come to the resolution of giving the regulation of their commerce to the federal head. I will venture to assert that there is not one of it's opposers who, placed on this ground, would not see the wisdom of this measure. The politics of Europe render it indispensably necessary that with respect to every thing external we be one nation only, firmly hooped together. Interior government is what each state should keep to itself. If it could be seen in Europe that all our states could be brought to concur in what the Virginia assembly has done, it would produce a total revolution in their opinion of us, and respect for us. And it should ever be held in mind that insult and war are the consequences of a want of respectability in the national character. As long as the states exercise separately those acts of power which respect foreign nations, so long will there continue to be irregularities committing by some one or other of them which will constantly keep us on an ill footing with foreign nations. . . .

"A CRUSADE AGAINST IGNORANCE" [4]

To George Wythe

Paris Aug 13, 1786

The European papers have announced that the assembly of Virginia were occupied on the revisal of their Code of laws. This, with some

[3] Boyd, IX, 264.
[4] Boyd, X, 244–45.

other similar intelligence, has contributed much to convince the people of Europe, that what the English papers are constantly publishing of our anarchy, is false; as they are sensible that such a work is that of a people only who are in perfect tranquillity. Our act for freedom of religion is extremely applauded. The Ambassadors and ministers of the several nations of Europe resident at this court have asked of me copies of it to send to their sovereigns, and it is inserted at full length in several books now in the press; among others, in the new Encyclopedie. I think it will produce considerable good even in these countries where ignorance, superstition, poverty and oppression of body and mind in every form, are so firmly settled on the mass of the people, that their redemption from them can never be hoped. If the almighty had begotten a thousand sons, instead of one, they would not have sufficed for this task. If all the sovereigns of Europe were to set themselves to work to emancipate the minds of their subjects from their present ignorance and prejudices, and that as zealously as they now endeavor the contrary, a thousand years would not place them on that high ground on which our common people are now setting out. Ours could not have been so fairly put into the hands of their own common sense, had they not been separated from their parent stock and been kept from contamination, either from them, or the other people of the old world, by the intervention of so wide an ocean. To know the worth of this, one must see the want of it here. I think by far the most important bill in our whole code is that for the diffusion of knowledge among the people. No other sure foundation can be devised for the preservation of freedom, and happiness. If any body thinks that kings, nobles, or priests are good conservators of the public happiness, send them here. It is the best school in the universe to cure them of that folly. They will see here with their own eyes that these descriptions of men are an abandoned confederacy against the happiness of the mass of people. The omnipotence of their effect cannot be better proved than in this country particularly, where notwithstanding the finest soil upon earth, the finest climate under heaven, and a people of the most benevolent, the most gay, and amiable character of which the human form is susceptible, where such a people I say, surrounded by so many blessings from nature, are yet loaded with misery by kings, nobles and priests, and by them alone. Preach, my dear Sir, a crusade against ignorance; establish and improve the law for educating the common people. Let our Countrymen know that the people alone can protect us against these evils, and that the tax which will be paid for this purpose is not more than the thousandth part of what will be paid to kings, priests and nobles who will rise up among us if we leave the people in ignorance. . . .

"A LITTLE REBELLION NOW AND THEN"[5]

To James Madison

Paris Jan. 30, 1787

. . . I am impatient to learn your sentiments on the late troubles in the Eastern states. So far as I have yet seen, they do not appear to threaten serious consequences. Those states have suffered by the stoppage of the channels of their commerce, which have not yet found other issues. This must render money scarce, and make the people uneasy. This uneasiness has produced acts absolutely unjustifiable: but I hope they will provoke no severities from their governments. A consciousness of those in power that their administration of the public affairs has been honest, may perhaps produce too great a degree of indignation: and those characters wherein fear predominates over hope may apprehend too much from these instances of irregularity. They may conclude too hastily that nature has formed man insusceptible of any other government but that of force, a conclusion not founded in truth, nor experience. Societies exist under three forms sufficiently distinguishable. 1. Without government, as among our Indians. 2. Under governments wherein the will of every one has a just influence, as is the case in England in a slight degree, and in our states in a great one. 3. Under governments of force: as is the case in all other monarchies and in most of the other republics. To have an idea of the curse of existence under these last, they must be seen. It is a government of wolves over sheep. It is a problem, not clear in my mind, that the 1st. condition is not the best. But I believe it to be inconsistent with any great degree of population. The second state has a great deal of good in it. The mass of mankind under that enjoys a precious degree of liberty and happiness. It has it's evils too: the principal of which is the turbulence to which it is subject. But weigh this against the oppressions of monarchy, and it becomes nothing. Malo periculosam, liberatem quam quietam servitutem. Even this evil is productive of good. It prevents the degeneracy of government, and nourishes a general attention to the public affairs. I hold it that a little rebellion now and then is a good thing, and as necessary in the political world as storms in the physical. Unsuccessful rebellions indeed generally es-

[5] Boyd, XI, 92–93, 94–95.

tablish the incroachments on the rights of the people which have produced them. An observation of this truth should render honest republican governors so mild in their punishment of rebellions, as not to discourage them too much. It is a medecine necessary for the sound health of government. . . .

As you are now returned into Congress it will become of importance that you should form a just estimate of certain public characters; on which therefore I will give you such notes as my knowledge of them has furnished me with. You will compare them with the materials you are otherwise possessed of, and decide on a view of the whole. You know the opinion I *formerly* entertained of *my friend Mr. Adams.* Yourself and the governor were the first who *shook* that opinion. I afterwards saw proofs which *convicted* him of a degree of *vanity,* and of a *blindness* to it, of which no germ *had appeared* in Congress. A 7-*months'* intimacy with him *here* and *as* many *weeks* in *London* have given me opportunities of studying him closely. *He is vain, irritable and a bad calculator of* the force and probable effect of the motives which govern men. This is *all* the *ill* which can possibly be *said of him.* He is as disinterested as the being which made him: he is profound in his views: and accurate in his judgment *except where knowledge of the world* is necessary to form a judgment. He is so amiable, that I pronounce you will love him if ever you become acquainted with him. He would be, as he was, a great man in *Congress.* . . .

ON THE NEW CONSTITUTION [6]

To James Madison

Paris Dec. 20, 1787

The season admitting only of operations in the Cabinet, and these being in a great measure secret, I have little to fill a letter. I will therefore make up the deficiency by adding a few words on the Constitution proposed by our Convention. I like much the general idea of framing a government which should go on of itself peaceably, without needing continual recurrence to the state lgeislatures. I like the organization of the government into Legislative, Judiciary and Executive. I like the power given the Legislature to levy taxes; and for that reason solely approve of the greater house being chosen by the people directly. For tho' I think a house chosen by them will be very illy qualified to legislate for the Union, for foreign nations &c.

[6] Boyd, XII, 439–42.

yet this evil does not weigh against the good of preserving inviolate the fundamental principle that the people are not to be taxed but by representatives chosen immediately by themselves. I am captivated by the compromise of the opposite claims of the great and little states, of the latter to equal, and the former to proportional influence. I am much pleased too with the substitution of the method of voting by persons, instead of that of voting by states: and I like the negative given to the Executive with a third of either house, though I should have liked it better had the Judiciary been associated for the purpose, or invested with a similar and separate power. There are other good things of less moment. I will now add what I do not like. First the omission of a bill of rights providing clearly and without the aid of sophisms for freedom of religion, freedom of the press, protection against standing armies, restriction against monopolies, the eternal and unremitting force of the habeas corpus laws, and trials by jury in all matters of fact triable by the laws of the land and not by the law of Nations. To say, as Mr. Wilson does that a bill of rights was not necessary because all is reserved in the case of the general government which is not given, while in the particular ones all is given which is not reserved might do for the Audience to whom it was addressed, but is surely gratis dictum, opposed by strong inferences from the body of the instrument, as well as from the omission of the clause of our present confederation which had declared that in express terms. It was a hard conclusion to say because there has been no uniformity among the states as to the cases triable by jury, because some have been so incautious as to abandon this mode of trial, therefore the more prudent states shall be reduced to the same level of calamity. It would have been much more just and wise to have concluded the other way that as most of the states had judiciously preserved this palladium, those who had wandered should be brought back to it, and to have established general right instead of general wrong. Let me add that a bill of rights is what the people are entitled to against every government on earth, general or particular, and what no just government should refuse, or rest on inference. The second feature I dislike, and greatly dislike, is the abandonment in every instance of the necessity of rotation in office, and most particularly in the case of the President. Experience concurs with reason in concluding that the first magistrate will always be re-elected if the constitution permits it. He is then an officer for life. . . . An incapacity to be elected a second time would have been the only effectual preventative. The power of removing him every fourth year by the vote of the people is a power which will not be exercised.

The king of Poland is removable every day by the Diet, yet he is never removed.—Smaller objections are the Appeal in fact as well as law, and the binding all persons Legislative, Executive and Judiciary by oath to maintain that constitution. I do not pretend to decide what would be the best method of procuring the establishment of the manifold good things in this constitution, and of getting rid of the bad. Whether by adopting it in hopes of future amendment, or, after it has been duly weighed and canvassed by the people, after seeing the parts they generally dislike, and those they generally approve, to say to them "We see now what you wish. Send together your deputies again, let them frame a constitution for you omitting what you have condemned, and establishing the powers you approve. Even these will be a great addition to the energy of your government."—At all events I hope you will not be discouraged from other trials, if the present one should fail of it's full effect.—I have thus told you freely what I like and dislike: merely as a matter of curiosity for I know your own judgment has been formed on all these points after having heard every thing which could be urged on them. I own I am not a friend to a very energetic government. It is always oppressive. The late rebellion in Massachusets has given more alarm than I think it should have done. Calculate that one rebellion in 13 states in the course of 11 years, is but one for each state in a century and a half. No country should be so long without one. Nor will any degree of power in the hands of government prevent insurrections. France with all it's despotism, and two or three hundred thousand men always in arms has had three insurrections in the three years I have been here in every one of which greater numbers were engaged than in Massachusetts and a great deal more blood was split. In Turkey, which Montesquieu supposes more despotic, insurrections are the events of every day. In England, where the hand of power is lighter than here, but heavier than with us they happen every half dozen years. Compare again the ferocious depredations of their insurgents with the order, the moderation and the almost self extinguishment of ours.—After all, it is my principle that the will of the Majority should always prevail. If they approve the proposed Convention in all it's parts, I shall concur in it chearfully, in hopes that they will amend it whenever they shall find it work wrong. I think our governments will remain virtuous for many centuries; as long as they are chiefly agricultural; and this will be as long as there shall be vacant lands in any part of America. When they get piled upon one another in large cities, as in Europe, they will become corrupt as in Europe. Above all things I hope the education of the common people will be attended to; convinced that on their good sense we may rely with the most security for the preservation of a due degree of liberty. I have tired you by this time with my disquisitions and will therefore only add assurances of the sincerity of those sentiments of esteem and attachment with which I am Dear Sir your affectionate friend & servant,

YOU CANNOT "ARRAY YOURSELF AGAINST THE PEOPLE" [7]

To Lafayette

Paris May 6, 1789

My Dear Friend

As it becomes more and more possible that the Noblesse will go wrong, I become uneasy for you. Your principles are decidedly with the tiers etat, and your instructions against them. A complaisance to the latter on some occasions and an adherence to the former on others, may give an appearance of trimming between the two parties which may lose you both. You will in the end go over wholly to the tiers etat, because it will be impossible for you to live in a constant sacrifice of your own sentiments to the prejudices of the Noblesse. But you would be received by the tiers etat at any future day, coldly and without confidence. It appears to me the moment to take at once that honest and manly stand with them which your own principles dictate. This will win their hearts for ever, be approved by the world which marks and honours you as the man of the people, and will be an eternal consolation to yourself. The Noblesse, and especially the Noblesse of Auvergne will always prefer men who will do their dirty work for them. You are not made for that. They will therefore soon drop you, and the people in that case will perhaps not take you up. Suppose a scission should take place. The priests and nobles will secede, the nation will remain in place and, with the king, will do it's own business. If violence should be attempted, where will you be? You cannot then take side with the people in opposition to your own vote, that very vote which will have helped to produce the scission. Still less can you array yourself against the people. That is impossible. Your instructions are indeed a difficulty. But to state this at it's worst, it is only a single difficulty, which a single effort surmounts. Your instructions can never embarrass you a second time, whereas an acquiescence under them will reproduce greater difficulties every day and without end. Besides, a thousand circumstances offer as many justifications

[7] Boyd, XV, 97–98.

of your departure from your instructions. Will it be impossible to persuade all parties that (as for good legislation two houses are necessary) the placing the privileged classes together in one house and the unprivileged in another, would be better for both than a scission. I own I think it would. People can never agree without some sacrifices; and it appears but a moderate sacrifice in each party to meet on this middle ground. The attempt to bring this about might satisfy your instructions, and a failure in it would justify your siding with the people even to those who think instructions are laws of conduct.— Forgive me, my dear friend, if my anxiety for you makes me talk of things I know nothing about. You must not consider this as advice. I know you and myself too well to presume to offer advice. Receive it merely, as the expression of my uneasiness and the effusion of that sincere friendship with which I am, my dear sir, Your's affectionately. . . .

THE FRENCH REVOLUTION [8]

To Richard Price

Paris July 12, 1789

Dear Sir

The delay of my Congé permits me still the pleasure of continuing to communicate the principal things which pass here. I have already informed you that the proceedings of the states general were tied up by the difficulty which arose as to the manner of voting, whether it should be by persons or orders. The Tiers at length gave an ultimate invitation to the other two orders to come and join them, informing them at the same time that if they did not they would proceed without them. The majority of the clergy joined them. The king then interposed by the seance royale of which you have heard. The decision he undertook to pronounce was declared null by the assembly and they proceeded in business. Tumults in Paris and Versailles and still more the declared defection of the Souldiery to the popular cause produced from the king an invitation to the Nobles and the minority of the clergy to go and join the common assembly. They did so, and since that time the three orders are in one room, voting by persons, and without any sensible dissension. Still the body of the nobles are rankling at the heart; but I see no reason to apprehend any great evil from it. Another appearance indeed, the approach of a great

[8] Boyd, XV, 271–72.

number of troops, principally foreigners, have given uneasiness. The
Assembly addressed the king in an eloquent and masculine stile. His
answer, tho' dry, disavows every object but that of keeping the two
capitals quiet. The States then are in quiet possession of the powers
of the nation, and have begun the great work of building up a constitution. They appointed a committee to arrange the order in which
they should proceed, and I will give you the arrangement, because it
will shew you they mean to begin the building at the bottom, and
know how to do it. They entitle it "Ordre du travail." . . .

The Declaration of the rights of man, which constitutes the 1st.
chapter of this work, was brought in the day before yesterday, and
referred to the bureaus. You will observe that these are the outlines
of a great work, and be assured that the body engaged in it are equal
to a masterly execution of it. They may meet with some difficulties
from within their body and some from without. There may be small
and temporary checks. But I think they will persevere to it's accomplishment. The mass of the people is with them: the effective part of
the clergy is with them: so I believe is the souldiery and a respectable
proportion of the officers. They have against them the high officers,
the high clergy, the noblesse and the parliaments. This you see is an
army of officers without souldiers. Should this revolution succeed, it
is the beginning of the reformation of the governments of Europe. . . .

"THE EARTH BELONGS TO THE LIVING"[9]

To James Madison

Paris September 6, 1789

I sit down to write to you without knowing by what occasion I
shall send my letter. I do it because a subject comes into my head which
I would wish to develope a little more than is practicable in the
hurry of the moment of making up general dispatches.

The question Whether one generation of men has a right to bind
another, seems never to have been stated either on this or our side
of the water. Yet it is a question of such consequences as not only to
merit decision, but place also, among the fundamental principles of
every government. The course of reflection in which we are immersed
here on the elementary principles of society has presented this question to my mind; and that no such obligation can be so transmitted I
think very capable of proof—I set out on this ground, which I sup-

[9] Boyd, XV, 392–97.

pose to be self evident, *"that the earth belongs in usufruct to the living"*: that the dead have neither powers nor rights over it. The portion occupied by any individual ceases to be his when himself ceases to be, and reverts to the society. If the society has formed no rules for the appropriation of it's lands in severalty, it will be taken by the first occupants. These will generally be the wife and children of the decedent. If they have formed rules of appropriation, those rules may give it to the wife and children, or to some one of them, or to the legatee of the deceased. So they may give it to his creditor. But the child, the legatee, or creditor takes it, not by any natural right, but by a law of the society of which they are members, and to which they are subject. Then no man can, by *natural right*, oblige the lands he occupied, or the persons who succeed him in that occupation, to the paiment of debts contracted by him. For if he could, he might, during his own life, eat up the usufruct of the lands for several generations to come, and then the lands would belong to the dead, and not to the living, which would be the reverse of our principle.

What is true of every member of the society individually, is true of them all collectively, since the rights of the whole can be no more than the sum of the rights of the individuals.—To keep our ideas clear when applying them to a multitude, let us suppose a whole generation of men to be born on the same day, to attain mature age on the same day, and to die on the same day, leaving a succeeding generation in the moment of attaining their mature age all together. Let the ripe age be supposed of 21. years, and their period of life 34. years more, that being the average term given by the bills of mortality to persons who have already attained 21. years of age. Each successive generation would, in this way, come on, and go off the stage at a fixed moment, as individuals do now. Then I say the earth belongs to each of these generations, during it's course, fully, and in their own right. The 2d. generation receives it clear of the debts and incumberances of the 1st. the 3d. of the 2d. and so on. For if the 1st. could charge it with a debt, then the earth would belong to the dead and not the living generation. Then no generation can contract debts greater than may be paid during the course of it's own existence. At 21. years of age they may bind themselves and their lands for 34. years to come: at 22. for 33: at 23. for 32. and at 54. for one year only; because these are the terms of life which remain to them at those respective epochs.—But a material difference must be noted between the succession of an individual, and that of a whole generation. Individuals are parts only of a society, subject to the laws of the whole. These laws may appropriate the portion of land occupied by a decedent to his creditor rather than to any other, or to his child on condition he satisfies the creditor. But when a whole generation, that is, the whole society dies, as in the case we have supposed, and another generation or society succeeds, this forms a whole, and there is no superior who can give their territory to a third society, who may have lent money to their predecessors beyond their faculties of paying.

What is true of a generation all arriving to self-government on the same day, and dying all on the same day, is true of those in a constant course of decay and renewal, with this only difference. A generation coming in and going out entire, as in the first case, would have a right in the 1st. year of their self-dominion to contract a debt for 33. years, in the 10th. for 24. in the 20th. for 14. in the 30th. for 4. whereas generations, changing daily by daily deaths and births, have one constant term, beginning at the date of their contract, and ending when a majority of those of full age at that date shall be dead. The length of that term may be estimated from the tables of mortality, corrected by the circumstances of climate, occupation &c. peculiar to the country of the contractors. Take, for instance, the table of M. de Buffon wherein he states 23,994 deaths, and the ages at which they happened. Suppose a society in which 23,994 persons are born every year, and live to the ages stated in this table. The conditions of that society will be as follows. 1st. It will consist constantly of 617,703. persons of all ages. 2ly. Of those living at any one instant of time, one half will be dead in 24. years 8. months. 3dly. 10,675 will arrive every year at the age of 21. years complete. 4ly. It will constantly have 348,417 persons of all ages above 21. years. 5ly. And the half of those of 21. years and upwards living at any one instant of time will be dead in 18. years 8. months, or say 19. years as the nearest integral number. Then 19. years is the term beyond which neither the representatives of a nation, nor even the whole nation itself assembled, can validly extend a debt. . . .

I suppose that the recieved opinion, that the public debts of one generation devolve on the next, has been suggested by our seeing habitually in private life that he who succeeds to lands is required to pay the debts of his ancestor or testator: without considering that this requisition is municipal only, not moral; flowing from the will of the society, which has found it convenient to appropriate lands, become vacant by the death of their occupant, on the condition of a paiment of his debts: but that between society and society, or generation and generation, there is no municipal obligation, no umpire but the law of nature. We seem not to have percieved that, by the law of nature, one generation is to another as one independant nation to another. . . .

On similar grounds it may be proved that no society can make a perpetual constitution, or even a perpetual law. The earth belongs always to the living generation. They may manage it then, and what proceeds from it, as they please, during their usufruct. They are masters too of their own persons, and consequently may govern them as they please. But persons and property make the sum of the objects of government. The constitution and the laws of their predecessors extinguished then in their natural course with those who gave them being. This could preserve that being till it ceased to be itself, and no longer. Every constitution then, and every law, naturally expires at the end of 19 years. If it be enforced longer, it is an act of force, and not of right.—It may be said that the succeeding generation exercising in fact the power of repeal, this leaves them as free as if the constitution or law had been expressly limited to 19 years only. In the first place, this objection admits the right, in proposing an equivalent. But the power of repeal is not an equivalent. It might be indeed if every form of government were so perfectly contrived that the will of the majority could always be obtained fairly and without impediment. But this is true of no form. The people cannot assemble themselves. Their representation is unequal and vicious. Various checks are opposed to every legislative proposition. Factions get possession of the public councils. Bribery corrupts them. Personal interests lead them astray from the general interests of their constituents: and other impediments arise so as to prove to every practical man that a law of limited duration is much more manageable than one which needs a repeal.

This principle that the earth belongs to the living, and not to the dead, is of very extensive application and consequences, in every country, and most especially in France. . . .

Turn this subject in your mind, my dear Sir, and particularly as to the power of contracting debts; and develope it with that perspicuity and cogent logic so peculiarly yours. Your station in the councils of our country gives you an opportunity of producing it to public consideration, of forcing it into discussion. At first blush it may be rallied, as a theoretical speculation: but examination will prove it to be solid and salutary. It would furnish matter for a fine preamble to our first law for appropriating the public revenue; and it will exclude at the threshold of our new government the contagious and ruinous errors of this quarter of the globe, which have armed despots with means, not sanctioned by nature, for binding in chains their fellow men. We have already given in example one effectual check to the Dog of war by transferring the power of letting him loose from the Executive to the Legislative body, from those who are to spend to those who are to pay. I should be pleased to see this second obstacle held out by us also in the first instance. No nation can make a declaration against the validity of long-contracted debts so disinterestedly as we, since we do not owe a shilling which may not be paid with ease, principal and interest, within the time of our own lives.—Establish the principle also in the new law to be passed for protecting copyrights and new inventions, by securing the exclusive right for 19. instead of 14. years. Besides familiarising us to this term, it will be an instance the more of our taking reason for our guide, instead of English precedent, the habit of which fetters us with all the political heresies of a nation equally remarkeable for it's early excitement from some errors, and long slumbering under others. . . .

5

The American Scene Again: The 1790s

Jefferson's return to America in early 1790 was intended to be a temporary visit to attend to his personal affairs, and renew his sense of the American scene before resuming his ministerial post in Paris. In fact, Jefferson was slated to become the first Secretary of State in America. President Washington had firmly decided upon his fellow Virginian, and Madison as well as other friends of Jefferson were determined to persuade him to stay. Thus, Jefferson's arrival in Virginia became the occasion for an enthusiastic official welcome by the "citizens of Albemarle County" to express their appreciation for his past services and to hint broadly that they hoped he would continue to serve his country (by which they meant accepting the post of Secretary of State, at home). Jefferson's eloquent reply included a memorable statement of his deepest political principle: that it rested with Americans now "to shew by example the sufficiency of human reason for the care of human affairs."

From the spring of 1790, Jefferson entered upon his fateful role as a political leader in the infant republic. His friendship with John Adams had already cooled before he took on the duties of the Secretary of State; and Jefferson recorded his distress at the degree of aristocratic and monarchist sentiment, ceremony, and political consolidation that had quickly developed with the establishment of the new Federal Government. The titanic battle with Hamilton and his cohorts, who represented the administration but presumed to regard that as identical with the government, developed early in Washington's first administration. Washington himself managed to rise above the most bitter popular suspicions, but Jefferson, in close conjunction with Madison, emerged as the great figure of the Republican opposition; and Hamilton and Adams (distrustful, and at arm's length) constituted the Federalist "in" leadership.

Jefferson's retirement from Washington's Cabinet turned out to be only a temporary return to his family and home, for his

*election as Vice-President in John Adams' administration, how-
ever much the "Veep" cherished the thought of a smooth partnership with his former friend, plunged him rapidly into the
heat of partisan politics. In this atmosphere, Congress passed the
reactionary Alien and Sedition Acts. This legislation was sufficiently broad in scope and susceptible of such harsh interpretation that the Republican politicians feared that they themselves
might be imprisoned, while "alien" visitors—especially French
intellectuals—hastened to book passage to Europe in flight from
the threat of detention that was boldly stated against them in
the laws. The attack on the printers of the leading Republican
newspapers, under the Sedition law, gave substance to the charge
of Federalist contempt for the liberties of a free people; and
Jefferson's success in the election was the first great instance of a
peaceful change of entire administration by its political opposition under the orderly procedure outlined in the Constitution.
Jefferson, who suffered through the agonizing delays over the
determination by Congress to recognize him as President and
Burr as Vice-President termed this complex chain of events "The
Revolution of 1800." He sincerely believed that the inroads made
on genuine republican principles and on the spirit of popular
self-government were now to be repaired, and "an Empire of
Liberty" would replace the imitative and antirepublican principles of government which his predecessors in the 1790s had
attempted to fasten upon the American people. These beliefs
are memorably formulated in Jefferson's first Inaugural Address.*

JEFFERSON'S RESPONSE TO THE ADDRESS OF WELCOME BY THE CITIZENS OF ALBEMARLE ON HIS RETURN FROM EUROPE [1]

February 12, 1790

Gentlemen

The testimony of esteem with which you are pleased to honour my return to my native country fills me with gratitude and pleasure. While it shews that my absence has not lost me your friendly recollection, it holds out the comfortable hope that when the hour of retirement shall come, I shall again find myself amidst those with whom I have long lived, with whom I wish to live, and whose affection is the source of my purest happiness. Their favor was the door thro' which I was ushered

[1] Boyd, XVI, 178–79.

on the stage of public life; and while I have been led on thro' it's varying scenes, I could not be unmindful of those who assigned me my first part.

My feeble and obscure exertions in their service, and in the holy cause of freedom, have had no other merit than that they were my best. We have all the same. We have been fellow-labourers and fellow-sufferers, and heaven has rewarded us with a happy issue from our struggles. It rests now with ourselves alone to enjoy in peace and concord the blessings of self-government, so long denied to mankind: to shew by example the sufficiency of human reason for the care of human affairs and that the will of the majority, the Natural law of every society, is the only sure guardian of the rights of man. Perhaps even this may sometimes err. But it's errors are honest, solitary and short-lived.—Let us then, my dear friends, for ever bow down to the general reason of the society. We are safe with that, even in it's deviations, for it soon returns again to the right way. These are lessons we have learnt together. We have prospered in their practice, and the liberality with which you are pleased to approve my attachment to the general rights of mankind assures me we are still together in these it's kindred sentiments.

Wherever I may be stationed, by the will of my country, it will be my delight to see, in the general tide of happiness, that yours too flows on in just place and measure. That it may flow thro' all times, gathering strength as it goes, and spreading the happy influence of reason and liberty over the face of the earth, is my fervent prayer to heaven.

"LESSONS IN REPUBLICANISM" [2]

To Thomas Paine

Philadelphia, June 19, 1792

Dear Sir,—I received with great pleasure the present of your pamphlets as well as for the thing itself as that it was a testimony of your recollection. Would you believe it possible that in this country there should be high & important characters who need your lessons in republicanism, & who do not heed them? It is but too true that we have a sect preaching up & pouting after an English constitution of king, lords, & commons, & whose heads are itching for crowns, coronets & mitres. But our people my good friend, are firm and unanimous in

[2] From *The Writings of Thomas Jefferson,* Paul Ford, ed. (New York: Knickerbocker Press, 1904), VII, 121–22.

their principles of republicanism & there is no better proof of it than that they love what you write and read it with delight. The printers season every newspaper with extracts from your last, as they did before from your first part of the *Rights of Man*. They have both served here to separate the wheat from the chaff, and to prove that tho' the latter appears on the surface, it is on the surface only. The bulk below is sound & pure. Go on then in doing with your pen what in other times was done with the sword: shew that reformation is more practicable by operating on the mind than on the body of man, and be assured that it has not a more sincere votary nor you a more ardent well-wisher than Yrs. &c.

ON THE HAMILTONIAN PROGRAM [3]

To the President of the United States

Monticello, September 9, 1792

. . . I now take the liberty of proceeding to that part of your letter wherein you notice the internal dissensions which have taken place within our government, and their disagreeable effect on its movements. That such dissensions have taken place is certain, and even among those who are nearest to you in the administration. To no one have they given deeper concern than myself; to no one equal mortification at being myself a part of them. Though I take to myself no more than my share of the general observations of your letter, yet I am so desirous ever that you should know the whole truth, and believe no more than the truth, that I am glad to seize every occasion of developing to you whatever I do or think relative to the government; and shall, therefore, ask permission to be more lengthy now than the occasion particularly calls for, or could otherwise perhaps justify.

When I embarked in the government, it was with a determination to intermeddle not at all with the Legislature, and as little as possible with my co-departments. . . . If it has been supposed that I have ever intrigued among the members of the Legislature to defeat the plans of the Secretary of the Treasury, it is contrary to all truth. As I never had the desire to influence the members, so neither had I any other means than my friendships, which I valued too highly to risk by usurpation on their freedom of judgment, and the conscientious pursuit of their own sense of duty. That I have utterly, in my private conversations, disapproved of the system of the Secretary of the

[3] Memorial Edition, VIII, 393–99.

Treasury, I acknowledge and avow; and this was not merely a speculative difference. His system flowed from principles adverse to liberty, and was calculated to undermine and demolish the Republic, by creating an influence of his department over the members of the Legislature. I saw this influence actually produced, and its first fruits to be the establishment of the great outlines of his project by the votes of the very persons who, having swallowed his bait, were laying themselves out to profit by his plans; and that had these persons withdrawn, as those interested in a question ever should, the vote of the disinterested majority was clearly the reverse of what they made it. These were no longer the votes then of the representatives of the people, but of deserters from the rights and interests of the people; and it was impossible to consider their decisions, which had nothing in view but to enrich themselves, as the measures of the fair majority, which ought always to be respected. If, what was actually doing, begat uneasiness in those who wished for virtuous government, what was further proposed was not less threatening to the friends of the Constitution. For, in a report on the subject of manufactures, (still to be acted on), it was expressly assumed that the General Government has a right to exercise all powers which may be for the *general welfare,* that is to say, all the legitimate powers of government; since no government has a legitimate right to do what is not for the welfare of the governed. There was, indeed, a sham limitation of the universality of this power *to cases where money is to be employed.* But about what is it that money cannot be employed? Thus the object of these plans, taken together, is to draw all the powers of government into the hands of the general Legislature, to establish means for corrupting a sufficient corps in that Legislature to divide the honest votes, and preponderate, by their own, the scale which suited, and to have the corps under the command of the Secretary of the Treasury, for the purpose of subverting, step by step, the principles of the Constitution which he has so often declared to be a thing of nothing, which must be changed. Such views might have justified something more than mere expressions of dissent, beyond which, nevertheless, I never went. Has abstinence from the department, committed to me, been equally observed by him? To say nothing of other interferences equally known, in the case of the two nations, with which we have the most intimate connections, France and England, my system was to give some satisfactory distinctions to the former, of little cost to us, in return for the solid advantages yielded us by them; and to have met the English with some restrictions which might induce them to abate their severities against our commerce. I have always supposed this coincided with your sentiments. Yet the Secretary of the Treasury, by his cabals with members of the Legislature, and by high-toned declamations on other occasions, has forced down his own system, which was exactly the reverse. He undertook, of his own authority, the conferences with the ministers of those two nations, and was, on every consultation, provided with some report of a conversation with the one or the other of them, adapted to his views. These views, thus made to prevail, their execution fell, of course, to me; and I can safely appeal to you, who have seen all my letters and proceedings, whether I have not carried them into execution as sincerely as if they had been my own, though I ever considered them as inconsistent with the honor and interest of our country. That they have been inconsistent with our interest is but too fatally proved by the stab to our navigation given by the French. So that if the question be by whose fault is it that Colonel Hamilton and myself have not drawn together? the answer will depend on that to two other questions, whose principles of administration best justify, by their purity, conscientious adherence? and which of us has, notwithstanding, stepped farthest into the control of the department of the other? . . .

REPUBLICAN HERESIES [4]

To Phillip Mazzei

Monticello, April 24, 1796

. . . The aspect of our politics has wonderfully changed since you left us. In place of that noble love of liberty and republican government which carried us triumphantly through the war, an Anglican monarchical aristocratical party has sprung up, whose avowed object is to draw over us the substance, as they have already done the forms, of the British government. The main body of our citizens, however, remain true to their republican principles; the whole landed interest is republican, and so is a great mass of talents. Against us are the Executive, the Judiciary, two out of three branches of the Legislature, all the officers of the government, all who want to be officers, all timid men who prefer the calm of despotism to the boisterous sea of liberty, British merchants and Americans trading on British capital, speculators and holders in the banks and public funds, a contrivance invented for the purposes of corruption, and for assimilating us in all things to the rotten as well as the sound parts of the British model. It would give you a fever were I to name to you the apostates who have gone

[4] Memorial Edition, IX, 335–36.

over to these heresies, men who were Samsons in the field and Solomons in the council, but who have had their heads shorn by the harlot England. In short, we are likely to preserve the liberty we have obtained only by unremitting labors and perils. But we shall preserve it; and our mass of weight and wealth on the good side is so great, as to leave no danger that force will ever be attempted against us. We have only to awake and snap the Lilliputian cords with which they have been entangling us during the first sleep which succeeded our labors. . . .

FIRST INAUGURAL ADDRESS, MARCH 4, 1801[5]

Friends and Fellow Citizens:—

Called upon to undertake the duties of the first executive office of our country, I avail myself of the presence of that portion of my fellow citizens which is here assembled, to express my grateful thanks for the favor with which they have been pleased to look toward me, to declare a sincere consciousness that the task is above my talents, and that I approach it with those anxious and awful presentiments which the greatness of the charge and the weakness of my powers so justly inspire. A rising nation, spread over a wise and fruitful land, traversing all the seas with the rich productions of their industry, engaged in commerce with nations who feel power and forget right, advancing rapidly to destinies beyond the reach of mortal eye—when I contemplate these transcendent objects, and see the honor, the happiness, and the hopes of this beloved country committed to the issue and the auspices of this day, I shrink from the contemplation, and humble myself before the magnitude of the undertaking. Utterly indeed, should I despair, did not the presence of many whom I here see remind me, that in the other high authorities provided by our constitution, I shall find resources of wisdom, of virtue, and of zeal, on which to rely under all difficulties. To you, then, gentlemen, who are charged with the sovereign functions of legislation, and to those associated with you, I look with encouragement for that guidance and support which may enable us to steer with safety the vessel in which we are all embarked amid the conflicting elements of a troubled world.

During the contest of opinion through which we have passed, the animation of discussion and of exertions has sometimes worn an aspect which might impose on strangers unused to think freely and to speak and to write what they think; but this being now decided by the

[5] Memorial Edition, III, 317–23.

voice of the nation, announced according to the rules of the constitution, all will, of course, arrange themselves under the will of the law, and unite in common efforts for the common good. All, too, will bear in mind this sacred principle, that though the will of the majority is in all cases to prevail, that will, to be rightful, must be reasonable; that the minority possess their equal rights, which equal laws must protect, and to violate which would be oppression. Let us, then, fellow citizens, unite with one heart and one mind. Let us restore to social intercourse that harmony and affection without which liberty and even life itself are but dreary things. And let us reflect that having banished from our land that religious intolerance under which mankind so long bled and suffered, we have yet gained little if we countenance a political intolerance as despotic, as wicked, and capable of as bitter and bloody persecutions. During the throes and convulsions of the ancient world, during the agonizing spasms of infuriated man, seeking through blood and slaughter his long-lost liberty, it was not wonderful that the agitations of the billows should reach even this distant and peaceful shore; that this should be more felt and feared by some and less by others; that this should divide opinion as to measures of safety. But every difference of opinion is not a difference of principle. We have called by different names brethren of the same principle. We are all republicans —we are all federalists. If there be any among us who would wish to dissolve this Union or to change its republican form, let them stand undisturbed as monuments of the safety with which error of opinion may be tolerated where reason is left free to combat it. I know, indeed, that some honest men fear that a republican government cannot be strong; that this government is not strong enough. But would the honest patriot, in the full tide of successful experiment, abandon a government which has so far kept us free and firm, on the theoretic and visionary fear that this government, the world's best hope, may by possibility want energy to preserve itself? I trust not. I believe this, on the contrary, the strongest government on earth. I believe it is the only one where every man, at the call of the laws, would fly to the standard of the law, and would meet invasions of the public order as his own personal concern. Sometimes it is said that man cannot be trusted with the government of himself. Can he, then, be trusted with the government of others? Or have we found angels in the forms of kings to govern him? Let history answer this question.

Let us, then, with courage and confidence pursue our own federal and republican principles, our attachment to our union and representative government. Kindly separated by nature and a wide ocean from the exterminating havoc of one quarter of the globe; too high-minded to endure the degradations of the others; possessing a chosen country, with room enough for our descendants to the hundredth and thousandth generation; entertaining a due sense of our equal right to the use of our own faculties, to the acquisitions of our industry, to honor and confidence from our fellow citizens, resulting not from birth but from our actions and their sense of them; enlightened by a benign religion, professed, indeed, and practiced in various forms, yet all of them including honesty, truth, temperance, gratitude, and the love of man; acknowledging and adoring an overruling Providence, which by all its dispensations proves that it delights in the happiness of man here and his greater happiness hereafter; with all these blessings, what more is necessary to make us a happy and prosperous people? Still one thing more, fellow citizens—a wise and frugal government, which shall restrain men from injuring one another, which shall leave them otherwise free to regulate their own pursuits of industry and improvement, and shall not take from the mouth of labor the bread it has earned. This is the sum of good government, and this is necessary to close the circle of our felicities.

About to enter, fellow citizens, on the exercise of duties which comprehend everything dear and valuable to you, it is proper that you should understand what I deem the essential principles of our government, and consequently those which ought to shape its administration. I will compress them within the narrowest compass they will bear, stating the general principle, but not all its limitations. Equal and exact justice to all men, of whatever state or persuasion, religious or political; peace, commerce, and honest friendship, with all nations —entangling alliances with none; the support of the state governments in all their rights, as the most competent administrations for our domestic concerns and the surest bulwarks against anti-republican tendencies; the preservation of the general government in its whole constitutional vigor, as the sheet anchor of our peace at home and safety abroad; a jealous care of the right of election by the people—a mild and safe corrective of abuses which are lopped by the sword of the revolution where peaceable remedies are unprovided; absolute acquiescence in the decisions of the majority—the vital principle of republics, from which there is no appeal but to force, the vital principle and immediate parent of despotism; a well-disciplined militia— our best reliance in peace and for the first moments of war, till regulars may relieve them; the supremacy of the civil over the military authority; economy in the public expense, that labor may be lightly burdened; the honest payment of our debts and sacred preservation of the public faith; encouragement of agriculture, and of commerce as its handmaid; the diffusion of information and the arraignment of all abuses at the bar of public reason; freedom of religion; freedom of the press; freedom of person under the protection of the habeas corpus; and trial by juries impartially selected—these principles form the bright constellation which has gone before us, and guided our steps through an age of revolution and reformation. The wisdom of our sages and the blood of our heroes have been devoted to their attainment. They should be the creed of our political faith—the text of civil instruction—the touchstone by which to try the services of those we trust; and should we wander from them in moments of error or alarm, let us hasten to retrace our steps and to regain the road which alone leads to peace, liberty, and safety.

I repair, then, fellow citizens, to the post you have assigned me. With experience enough in subordinate offices to have seen the difficulties of this, the greatest of all, I have learned to expect that it will rarely fall to the lot of imperfect man to retire from this station with the reputation and the favor which bring him into it. Without pretensions to that high confidence reposed in our first and great revolutionary character, whose pre-eminent services had entitled him to the first place in his country's love, and destined for him the fairest page in the volume of faithful history, I ask so much confidence only as may give firmness and effect to the legal administration of your affairs. I shall often go wrong through defect of judgment. When right, I shall often be thought wrong by those whose positions will not command a view of the whole ground. I ask your indulgence for my own errors, which will never be intentional; and your support against the errors of others, who may condemn what they would not if seen in all its parts. The approbation implied by your suffrage is a consolation to me for the past; and my future solicitude will be to retain the good opinion of those who have bestowed it in advance, to conciliate that of others by doing them all the good in my power, and to be instrumental to the happiness and freedom of all.

Relying, then, on the patronage of your good will, I advance with obedience to the work, ready to retire from it whenever you become sensible how much better choice it is in your power to make. And may that Infinite Power which rules the destinies of the universe, lead our councils to what is best, and give them a favorable issue for your peace and prosperity.

6
Morality and Education

Throughout his life, Jefferson continued to reflect deeply on matters of morality and education. On the basis of extended reading as well as experience he formed a view of both. He embodied his thoughts in numerous letters and reports, many of them essays in length; the collection of them would easily fill a volume. The three brief selections below will indicate something of the tenor of his thoughts. The first, to Peter Carr, is one of a series of advisory letters that Jefferson sent to young kinsmen and friends, providing guides for their education and morality. The second, to William Green Mumford, is one of this series but acquires unusual significance in that it bears on the critical climate of reaction created by the Alien and Sedition Acts, and permits Jefferson to reaffirm the faith and responsibilities of a champion of intellectual freedom. The third, to Benjamin Rush, takes up the important subject of "the morals of Jesus"—a subject about which Jefferson intended to write a book, and did manage even under the pressure of his Presidential duties to write several lengthy discussions and outlines.

"AN HONEST HEART . . . A KNOWING HEAD"[1]

To Peter Carr

Paris Aug. 19, 1785

Dear Peter

I received by Mr. Mazzei your letter of April 20. I am much mortified to hear that you have lost so much time, and that when you arrived in Williamsburgh you were not at all advanced from what you were when you left Monticello. Time now begins to be precious to you. Every day you lose, will retard a day your entrance on that public stage whereon you may begin to be useful to yourself. However the way to repair the loss is to improve the future time. I trust that with

[1] Boyd, VIII, 405–408.

your dispositions even the acquisition of science is a pleasing employment. I can assure you that the possession of it is what (next to an honest heart) will above all things render you dear to your friends, and give you fame and promotion in your own country. When your mind shall be well improved with science, nothing will be necessary to place you in the highest points of view but to pursue the interests of your country, the interests of your friends, and your own interests also with the purest integrity, the most chaste honour. The defect of these virtues can never be made up by all the other acquirements of body and mind. Make these then your first object. Give up money, give up fame, give up science, give the earth itself and all it contains rather than do an immoral act. And never suppose that in any possible situation or under any circumstances that it is best for you to do a dishonourable thing however slightly so it may appear to you. Whenever you are to do a thing tho' it can never be known but to yourself, ask yourself how you would act were all the world looking at you, and act accordingly. Encourage all your virtuous dispositions, and exercise them whenever an opportunity arises, being assured that they will gain strength by exercise as a limb of the body does, and that exercise will make them habitual. From the practice of the purest virtue you may be assured you will derive the most sublime comforts in every moment of life and in the moment of death. If ever you find yourself environed with difficulties and perplexing circumstances, out of which you are at a loss how to extricate yourself, do what is right, and be assured that that will extricate you the best out of the worst situations. Tho' you cannot see when you fetch one step, what will be the next, yet follow truth, justice, and plain-dealing, and never fear their leading you out of the labyrinth in the easiest manner possible. The knot which you thought a Gordian one will untie itself before you. Nothing is so mistaken as the supposition that a person is to extricate himself from a difficulty, by intrigue, by chicanery, by dissimulation, by trimming, by an untruth, by an injustice. This increases the difficulties tenfold, and those who pursue these methods, get themselves so involved at length that they can turn no way but their infamy becomes more exposed. It is of great importance to set a resolution, not to be shaken, never to tell an untruth. There is no vice so mean, so pitiful, so contemptible and he who permits himself to tell a lie once, finds it much easier to do it a second and third time, till at length it becomes habitual, he tells lies without attending to it, and truths without the world's believing him. This falsehood of the tongue leads to that of the heart, and in time depraves all it's good dispositions.

An honest heart being the first blessing, a knowing head is the second. It is time for you now to begin to be choice in your reading, to begin to pursue a regular course in it and not to suffer yourself to be turned to the right or left by reading any thing out of that course. I have long ago digested a plan for you, suited to the circumstances in which you will be placed. This I will detail to you from time to time as you advance. For the present I advise you to begin a course of antient history, reading every thing in the original and not in translations. First read Goldsmith's history of Greece. This will give you a digested view of that field. Then take up antient history in the detail, reading the following books in the following order. Herodotus. Thucydides. Xenophontis hellenica. Xenophontis Ababasis. Quintus Curtius. Justin. This shall form the first stage of your historical reading, and is all I need mention to you now. The next will be of Roman history. From that we will come down to Modern history. In Greek and Latin poetry, you have read or will read at school Virgil, Terence, Horace, Anacreon, Theocritus, Homer. Read also Milton's paradise lost, Ossian, Pope's works, Swift's works in order to form your style in your own language. In morality read Epictetus, Xenophontis memorabilia, Plato's Socratic dialogues, Cicero's philosophies. In order to assure a certain progress in this reading, consider what hours you have free from the school and the exercises of the school. Give about two of them every day to exercise; for health must not be sacrificed to learning. A strong body makes the mind strong. As to the species of exercise, I advise the gun. While this gives a moderate exercise to the body, it gives boldness, enterprize, and independance to the mind. Games played with the ball and others of that nature, are too violent for the body and stamp no character on the mind. Let your gun therefore be the constant companion of your walks. Never think of taking a book with you. The object of walking is to relax the mind. You should therefore not permit yourself even to think while you walk. But divert your attention by the objects surrounding you. Walking is the best possible exercise. Habituate yourself to walk very far. The Europeans value themselves on having subdued the horse to the uses of man. But I doubt whether we have not lost more than we have gained by the use of this animal. No one has occasioned so much the degeneracy of the human body. An Indian goes on foot nearly as far in a day, for a long journey, as an enfeebled white does on his horse, and he will tire the best horses. There is no habit you will value so much as that of walking far without fatigue. I would advise you to take your exercise in the afternoon. Not because it is the best time for exercise for certainly it is not; but because it is the best time to spare from your studies; and habit will soon reconcile it to health, and render it nearly as useful as if you gave to that the more precious hours of the day. A little walk of half an hour in the morning when you first rise is adviseable also. It shakes off sleep, and produces other good effects in the animal œconomy. Rise at a fixed and an early hour, and go to bed at a fixed and early hour also. Sitting up late at night is injurious to the health, and not useful to the mind.—Having ascribed proper hours to exercise, divide what remain (I mean of your vacant hours) into three portions. Give the principal to history, the other two, which should be shorter, to Philosophy and Poetry. Write me once every month or two and let me know the progress you make. Tell me in what manner you employ every hour in the day. The plan I have proposed for you is adapted to your present situation only. When that is changed, I shall propose a corresponding change of plan. I have ordered the following books to be sent to you from London to the care of Mr. Madison. Herodotus. Thucydides. Xenophon's Hellenics, Anabasis, and Memorabilia. Cicero's works. Barretti's Spanish and English dictionary. Martin's philosophical grammar and Martin's philosophia Britannica. I will send you the following from hence. Bezout's mathematics. De la Lande's astronomy. Muschenbroek's physics. Quintus Curtius. Justin, a Spanish grammar, and some Spanish books. You will observe that Martin, Bezout, De la Lande and Muschenbroek are not in the preceding plan. They are not to be opened till you go to the University. You are now I expect learning French. You must push this: because the books which will be put into your hands when you advance into Mathematics, Natural philosophy, Natural history, &c. will be mostly French, these sciences being better treated by the French than the English writers. Our future connection with Spain renders that the most necessary of the modern languages, after the French. When you become a public man you may have occasion for it, and the circumstance of your possessing that language may give you a preference over other candidates. I have nothing further to add for the present, than to husband well your time, cherish your instructors, strive to make every body your friend, & be assured that nothing will be so pleasing as your success. . . .

"THE FREEDOM OF THE HUMAN MIND" [2]

To William Green Mumford

Monticello June 18, 1799

Dear Sir,

I have to acknolege the reciept of your favor of May 14. in which you mention that you have finished the 6. first books of Euclid, plane trigonometry, surveying and algebra and ask whether I think a further pursuit of that branch of science would be useful to you. There are some propositions in the latter books of Euclid, and some of Archimedes, which are useful, and I have no doubt you have been made acquainted with them. Trigonometry, so far as this, is most valuable to every man, there is scarcely a day in which he will not resort to it for some of the purposes of common life. The science of calculation also is indispensible as far as the extraction of the square and cube roots; Algebra as far as the quadratic equation and the use of logarithms are often of value in ordinary cases: but all beyond these is but a luxury; a delicious luxury indeed; but not to be indulged in by one who is to have a profession to follow for his subsistence. In this light I view the conic sections, curves of the higher orders, perhaps even spherical trigonometry, Algebraical operations beyond the 2d dimension, and fluxions. There are other branches of science however worth the attention of every man: astronomy, botany, chemistry, natural philosophy, natural history, anatomy. Not indeed to be a proficient in them; but to possess their general principles and outlines, so as that we may be able to amuse and inform ourselves further in any of them as we proceed through life and have occasion for them. Some knowledge of them is necessary for our character as well as comfort. The general elements of astronomy and of natural philosophy are best acquired at an academy where we can have the benefit of the instruments and apparatus usually provided there: but the others may well be acquired from books alone as far as our purposes require. I have indulged myself in these observations to you, because the evidence cannot be unuseful to you of a person who has often had occasion to consider which of his acquisitions in science have been really useful to him in life, and which of them have been merely a matter of luxury.

[2] From Achille J. St. Onge, *Thomas Jefferson on Science and Freedom,* with a foreword by Julian Boyd (Worcester, 1964), pp. 47–60.

I am among those who think well of the human character generally. I consider man as formed for society, and endowed by nature with those dispositions which fit him for society. I believe also, with Condorcet, as mentioned in your letter, that his mind is perfectible to a degree of which we cannot as yet form any conception. It is impossible for a man who takes a survey of what is already known, not to see what an immensity in every branch of science yet remains to be discovered, and that too of articles to which our faculties seem adequate. In geometry and calculation we know a great deal. Yet there are some desiderata. In anatomy great progress has been made; but much is still to be acquired. In natural history we possess knowledge; but we want a great deal. In chemistry we are not yet sure of the first elements. Our natural philosophy is in a very infantine state; perhaps for great advances in it, a further progress in chemistry is necessary. Surgery is well advanced; but prodigiously short of what may be. The state of medicine is worse than that of total ignorance. Could we divest ourselves of every thing we suppose we know in it, we should start from a higher ground and with fairer prospects. From Hippocrates to Brown we have had nothing but a succession of hypothetical systems each having it's day of vogue, like the fashions and fancies of caps and gowns, and yielding in turn to the next caprice. Yet the human frame, which is to be the subject of suffering and torture under these learned modes, does not change. We have a few medecines, as the bark, opium, mercury, which in a few well defined diseases are of unquestionable virtue: but the residuary list of the materia medica, long as it is, contains but the charlataneries of the art; and of the diseases of doubtful form, physicians have ever had a false knowledge, worse than ignorance. Yet surely the list of unequivocal diseases and remedies is capable of enlargement; and it is still more certain that in the other branches of science, great fields are yet to be explored to which our faculties are equal, and that to an extent of which we cannot fix the limits. I join you therefore in branding as cowardly the idea that the human mind is incapable of further advances. This is precisely the doctrine which the present despots of the earth are inculcating, and their friends here re-echoing; and applying especially to religion and politics; "that it is not probable that any thing better will be discovered than what was known to our fathers." We are to look backwards then and not forwards for the improvement of science, and to find it amidst feudal barbarians and the fires of Spital-fields. But thank heaven the American mind is already too much opened, to listen to these impostures; and while the art of printing is left to us, science can never be retrograde; what is once acquired of real knowlege can never be lost. To preserve the freedom of the human mind then and freedom of the press, every spirit should be ready to devote itself to martyrdom; for as long as we may think as we will, and speak as we think, the condition of man will proceed in improvement. The generation which is going off the stage has deserved well of mankind for the struggles it has made, and for having arrested that course of despotism which had overwhelmed the world for thousands and thousands of years. If there seems to be danger that the ground they have gained will be lost again, that danger comes from the generation your contemporary. But that the enthusiasm which characterises youth should lift its parricide hands against freedom and science, would be such a monstrous phænomenon as I cannot place among possible things in this age and this country. Your college at least has shewn itself incapable of it; and if the youth of any other place have seemed to rally under other banners it has been from delusions which they will soon dissipate. I shall be happy to hear from you from time to time, and of your progress in study, and to be useful to you in whatever is in my power. . . .

THE MORALS OF JESUS

To Doctor Benjamin Rush[3]

Washington, April 21, 1803

Dear Sir,—In some of the delightful conversations with you, in the evenings of 1798–99, and which served as an anodyne to the afflictions of the crisis through which our country was then laboring, the Christian religion was sometimes our topic; and I then promised you, that one day or other, I would give you my views of it. They are the result of a life of inquiry and reflection, and very different from that anti-Christian system imputed to me by those who know nothing of my opinions. To the corruptions of Christianity I am, indeed, opposed; but not to the genuine precepts of Jesus himself. I am a Christian, in the only sense in which he wished any one to be; sincerely attached to his doctrines, in preference to all others; ascribing to himself every *human* excellence; and believing he never claimed any other. At the short interval since these conversations, when I could justifiably abstract my mind from public affairs, the subject has been under my contemplation. But the more I considered it, the more it expanded beyond the measure of either my time or information. In the moment

[3] Memorial Edition, X, 379–85.

of my late departure from Monticello, I received from Dr. Priestley, his little treatise of "Socrates and Jesus Compared." This being a section of the general view I had taken of the field, it became a subject of reflection while on the road, and unoccupied otherwise. The result was, to arrange in my mind a syllabus, or outline of such an estimate of the comparative merits of Christianity, as I wished to see executed by some one of more leisure and information for the task, than myself. This I now send you, as the only discharge of my promise I can probably ever execute. And in confiding it to you, I know it will not be exposed to the malignant perversions of those who make every word from me a text for new misrepresentations and calumnies. I am moreover averse to the communication of my religious tenets to the public; because it would countenance the presumption of those who have endeavored to draw them before that tribunal, and to seduce public opinion to erect itself into that inquisition over the rights of conscience, which the laws have so justly proscribed. It behooves every man who values liberty of conscience for himself, to resist invasions of it in the case of others; or their case may, by change of circumstances, become his own. It behooves him, too, in his own case, to give no example of concession, betraying the common right of independent opinion, by answering questions of faith, which the laws have left between God and himself. Accept my affectionate salutations.

Syllabus of an Estimate of the Merit of the Doctrines of Jesus, compared with those of others

In a comparative view of the Ethics of the enlightened nations of antiquity, of the Jews and of Jesus, no notice should be taken of the corruptions of reason among the ancients, to wit, the idolatry and superstition of the vulgar, nor of the corruptions of Christianity by the learned among its professors.

Let a just view be taken of the moral principles inculcated by the most esteemed of the sects of ancient philosophy, or of their individuals; particularly Pythagoras, Socrates, Epicurus, Cicero, Epictetus, Seneca, Antoninus.

I. Philosophers. 1. Their precepts related chiefly to ourselves, and the government of those passions which, unrestrained, would disturb our tranquillity of mind.[4] In this branch of philosophy they were really great.

---

[4] To explain, I will exhibit the heads of Seneca's and Cicero's philosophical works, the most extensive of any we have received from the ancients. Of ten heads in Seneca, seven relate to ourselves, viz. *de ira, consolatio, de tranquilitate, de*

2. In developing our duties to others, they were short and defective. They embraced, indeed, the circle of kindred and friends, and inculcated patriotism, or the love of our country in the aggregate, as a primary obligation: towards our neighbors and countrymen they taught justice, but scarcely viewed them as within the circle of benevolence. Still less have they inculcated peace, charity and love to our fellow men, or embraced with benevolence the whole family of mankind.

II. Jews. 1. Their system was Deism; that is, the belief in one only God. But their ideas of him and of his attributes were degrading and injurious.

2. Their Ethics were not only imperfect, but often irreconcilable with the sound dictates of reason and morality, as they respect intercourse with those around us; and repulsive and anti-social, as respecting other nations. They needed reformation, therefore, in an eminent degree.

III. Jesus. In this state of things among the Jews, Jesus appeared. His parentage was obscure; his condition poor; his education null; his natural endowments great; his life correct and innocent: he was meek, benevolent, patient, firm, disinterested, and of the sublimest eloquence.

The disadvantages under which his doctrines appear are remarkable.

1. Like Socrates and Epictetus, he wrote nothing himself.

2. But he had not, like them, a Xenophon or an Arrian to write for him. I name not Plato, who only used the name of Socrates to cover the whimsies of his own brain. On the contrary, all the learned of his country, entrenched in its power and riches, were opposed to him, lest his labors should undermine their advantages; and the committing to writing his life and doctrines fell on unlettered and ignorant men; who wrote, too, from memory, and not till long after the transactions had passed.

3. According to the ordinary fate of those who attempt to enlighten and reform mankind, he fell an early victim to the jealousy and combination of the altar and the throne, at about thirty-three years of age, his reason having not yet attained the *maximum* of its energy, nor the course of his preaching, which was but of three years at most, presented occasions for developing a complete system of morals.

---

constantia sapientis, de otio sapientis, de vita beata, de brevitate vitae; two relate to others, *de clementia, de beneficiis;* and one relates to the government of the world, *de providentia.* Of eleven tracts of Cicero, five respect ourselves, viz. *de finibus, Tusculana, academica, paradoxa, de Senectute;* one, *de officiis,* relates partly to ourselves, partly to others; one, *de amicitia,* relates to others; and four are on different subjects, to wit, *de natura deorum, de divinatione, de fato,* and *somnium Scipionis.* [Jefferson's footnote.]

4. Hence the doctrines which he really delivered were defective as a whole, and fragments only of what he did deliver have come to us mutilated, misstated, and often unintelligible.

5. They have been still more disfigured by the corruptions of schismatizing followers, who have found an interest in sophisticating and perverting the simple doctrines he taught, by engrafting on them the mysticisms of a Grecian sophist, frittering them into subtleties, and obscuring them with jargon, until they have caused good men to reject the whole in disgust, and to view Jesus himself as an impostor.

IV. Notwithstanding these disadvantages, a system of morals is presented to us, which, if filled up in the style and spirit of the rich fragments he left us, would be the most perfect and sublime that has ever been taught by man.

The question of his being a member of the Godhead, or in direct communication with it, claimed for him by some of his followers, and denied by others, is foreign to the present view, which is merely an estimate of the intrinsic merits of his doctrines.

1. He corrected the Deism of the Jews, confirming them in their belief of one only God, and giving them juster notions of his attributes and government.

2. His moral doctrines, relating to kindred and friends, were more pure and perfect than those of the most correct of the philosophers, and greatly more so than those of the Jews; and they went far beyond both in inculcating universal philanthropy, not only to kindred and friends, to neighbors and countrymen, but to all mankind, gathering all into one family, under the bonds of love, charity, peace, common wants and common aids. A development of this head will evince the peculiar superiority of the system of Jesus over all others.

3. The precepts of philosophy, and of the Hebrew code, laid hold of actions only. He pushed his scrutinies into the heart of man; erected his tribunal in the region of his thoughts, and purified the waters at the fountain head.

4. He taught, emphatically, the doctrines of a future state, which was either doubted, or disbelieved by the Jews; and wielded it with efficacy, as an important incentive, supplementary to the other motives to moral conduct.

7
Statesman in Retirement, 1809-1826

When Jefferson retired from active political affairs and could return to his beloved Monticello—to ride, read, experiment with crops, and draw architectural plans—he devoted himself to founding the University of Virginia and to reviewing the meaning of the American experiment in free government. One phase of this was reflected in his renewed friendship with John Adams, with whom he carried on a brilliant epistolary debate on their views and efforts in behalf the principles of 1776 —now tested by more than three decades of Amercan and European experience. The three selections below will illustrate the rich intellectual texture of Jefferson's older years.

In addition, each urgent issue of the day elicited his keen and powerful comment and analysis. From this wide range of correspondence, the selections below show Jefferson's later thinking on the subjects of manufactures, slavery, and the relationship between liberty and learning. The final selection, written in the last month of his life, and a half century after the Declaration of Independence, reaffirms his abiding faith in its principles of human rights.

ON ADAMS [1]

To Dr. Benjamin Rush

Monticello, January 16, 1811

. . . I receive with sensibility your observations on the discontinuance of friendly correspondence between Mr. Adams and myself, and the concern you take in its restoration. The discontinuance has not proceeded from me, nor from the want of sincere desire and of effort on my part, to renew our intercourse. You know the perfect

[1] Memorial Edition, XIII, 2–9.

coincidence of principle and of action, in the early part of the Revolution, which produced a high degree of mutual respect and esteem between Mr. Adams and myself. Certainly no man was ever truer than he was, in that day, to those principles of rational republicanism which, after the necessity of throwing off our monarchy, dictated all our efforts in the establishment of a new government. And although he swerved, afterwards, towards the principles of the English constitution, our friendship did not abate on that account. While he was Vice-President, and I Secretary of State, I received a letter from President Washington, then at Mount Vernon, desiring me to call together the Heads of departments, and to invite Mr. Adams to join us (which, by-the-by, was the only instance of that being done) in order to determine on some measure which required despatch; and he desired me to act on it, as decided, without again recurring to him. I invited them to dine with me, and after dinner, sitting at our wine, having settled our question, other conversation came on, in which a collision of opinion arose between Mr. Adams and Colonel Hamilton, on the merits of the British constitution, Mr. Adams giving it as his opinion, that, if some of its defects and abuses were corrected, it would be the most perfect constitution of government ever devised by man. Hamilton, on the contrary, asserted, that with its existing vices, it was the most perfect model of government that could be formed; and that the correction of its vices would render it an impracticable government. And this you may be assured was the real line of difference between the political principles of these two gentlemen. Another incident took place on the same occasion, which will further delineate Mr. Hamilton's political principles. The room being hung around with a collection of the portraits of remarkable men, among them were those of Bacon, Newton and Locke, Hamilton asked me who they were. I told him they were my trinity of the three greatest men the world had ever produced, naming them. He paused for some time: "the greatest man," said he, "that ever lived, was Julius Cæsar." Mr. Adams was honest as a politician, as well as a man; Hamilton honest as a man, but, as a politician, believing in the necessity of either force or corruption to govern men.

You remember the machinery which the federalists played off, about that time, to beat down the friends to the real principles of our Constitution, to silence by terror every expression in their favor, to bring us into war with France and alliance with England, and finally to homologize our Constitution with that of England. Mr. Adams, you know, was overwhelmed with feverish addresses, dictated by the fear, and often by the pen, of the *bloody buoy,* and was seduced by them into some open indications of his new principles of government, and in fact, was so elated as to mix with his kindness a little supercilious-ness towards me. Even Mrs. Adams, with all her good sense and pru-dence, was sensibly flushed. And you recollect the short suspension of our intercourse, and the circumstance which gave rise to it, which you were so good as to bring to an early explanation, and have set to rights, to the cordial satisfaction of us all. The nation at length passed condemnation on the political principles of the federalists, by refusing to continue Mr. Adams in the Presidency. On the day on which we learned in Philadelphia the vote of the city of New York, which it was well known would decide the vote of the State, and that, again, the vote of the Union, I called on Mr. Adams on some official business. He was very sensibly affected, and accosted me with these words: "Well, I understand that you are to beat me in this contest, and I will only say that I will be as faithful a subject as any you will have." "Mr. Adams," said I, "this is no personal contest between you and me. Two systems of principles on the subject of government divide our fellow citizens into two parties. With one of these you concur, and I with the other. As we have been longer on the public stage than most of those now living, our names happen to be more generally known. One of these parties, therefore, has put your name at its head, the other mine. Were we both to die to-day, to-morrow two other names would be in the place of ours, without any change in the motion of the machinery. Its motion is from its principle, not from you or my-self." "I believe you are right," said he, "that we are but passive instru-ments, and should not suffer this matter to affect our personal disposi-tions." But he did not long retain this just view of the subject. I have always believed that the thousand calumnies which the federalists, in bitterness of heart, and mortification at their ejection, daily invented against me, were carried to him by their busy intriguers, and made some impression. When the election between Burr and myself was kept in suspense by the federalists, and they were meditating to place the President of the Senate at the head of the government, I called on Mr. Adams with a view to have this desperate measure prevented by his negative. He grew warm in an instant, and said with a vehemence he had not used towards me before, "Sir, the event of the election is within your own power. You have only to say you will do justice to the public creditors, maintain the navy, and not disturb those hold-ing offices, and the government will instantly be put into your hands. We know it is the wish of the people it should be so." "Mr. Adams," said I, "I know not what part of my conduct, in either public or private life, can have authorized a doubt of my fidelity to the public engagements. I say, however, I will not come into the government by capitulation. I will not enter on it, but in perfect freedom to follow the dictates of my own judgment." I had before given the same answer to the same intimation from Gouverneur Morris. "Then," said he, "things must take their course." I turned the conversation to something else, and soon took my leave. It was the first time in our lives we had ever parted with anything like dissatisfaction. And then followed those scenes of midnight appointment, which have been condemned by all men. The last day of his political power, the last hours, and even beyond the midnight, were employed in filling all offices, and especially permanent ones, with the bitterest federalists, and providing for me the alternative, either to execute the government by my enemies, whose study it would be to thwart and defeat all my measures, or to incur the odium of such numerous removals from office, as might bear me down. A little time and reflection effaced in my mind this temporary dissatisfaction with Mr. Adams, and restored me to that just estimate of his virtues and passions, which a long acquaintance had enabled me to fix. And my first wish became that of making his retirement easy by any means in my power; for it was understood he was not rich. I suggested to some republican members of the delegation from his State, the giving him, either directly or indirectly, an office, the most lucrative in that State, and then offered to be resigned, if they thought he would not deem it affrontive. They were of opinion he would take great offence at the offer; and moreover, that the body of republicans would consider such a step in the outset as auguring very ill of the course I meant to pursue. I dropped the idea, therefore, but did not cease to wish for some opportunity of renewing our friendly understanding. . . .

I have the same good opinion of Mr. Adams which I ever had. I know him to be an honest man, an able one with his pen, and he was a powerful advocate on the floor of Congress. He has been alienated from me, by belief in the lying suggestions contrived for electioneering purposes, that I perhaps mixed in the activity and intrigues of the occasion. My most intimate friends can testify that I was perfectly passive. They would sometimes, indeed, tell me what was going on; but no man ever heard me take part in such conversations; and none ever misrepresented Mr. Adams in my presence, without my asserting his just character. With very confidential persons I have doubtless disapproved of the principles and practices of his administration. This was unavoidable. But never with those with whom it could do him any injury. Decency would have required this conduct from me, if disposition had not; and I am satisfied Mr. Adams' conduct was equally honorable towards me. But I think it part of his character to suspect foul play in those of whom he is jealous, and not easily to relinquish his suspicions. . . .

ON PARTIES [2]

To John Adams

Monticello, June 27, 1813

. . . Men have differed in opinion, and been divided into parties by these opinions, from the first origin of societies, and in all governments where they have been permitted freely to think and to speak. The same political parties which now agitate the United States, have existed through all time. Whether the power of the people or that of the aristoi should prevail, were questions which kept the States of Greece and Rome in eternal convulsions, as they now schismatize every people whose minds and mouths are not shut up by the gag of a despot. And in fact, the terms of whig and tory belong to natural as well as to civil history. They denote the temper and constitution of mind of different individuals. To come to our own country, and to the times when you and I became first acquainted, we well remember the violent parties which agitated the old Congress, and their bitter contests. There you and I were together, and the Jays, and the Dickinsons, and other anti-independents, were arrayed against us. They cherished the monarchy of England, and we the rights of our countrymen. When our present government was in the mew, passing from Confederation to Union, how bitter was the schism between the Feds and Antis! Here you and I were together again. For although, for a moment, separated by the Atlantic from the scene of action, I favored the opinion that nine States should confirm the constitution, in order to secure it, and the others hold off until certain amendments, deemed favorable to freedom, should be made. I rallied in the first instant to the wiser proposition of Massachusetts, that all should confirm, and then all instruct their delegates to urge those amendments. The amendments were made, and all were reconciled to the government. But as soon as it was put into motion, the line of division was again drawn. We broke into two parties, each wishing to give the government a different direction; the one to strengthen the most popular branch, the other the more permanent branches, and to extend their permanence. Here you and I separated for the first time, and as we had been longer than most others on the public theatre, and our names therefore were more

[2] Memorial Edition, XIII, 279–81.

familiar to our countrymen the party which considered you as thinking with them, placed your name at their head; the other, for the
same reason, selected mine. But neither decency nor inclination permitted us to become the advocates of ourselves, or to take part personally in the violent contests which followed. We suffered ourselves,
as you so well expressed it, to be passive subjects of public discussion. . . .

NATURAL ARISTOCRACY [3]

To John Adams

Monticello, October 28, 1813

. . . I agree with you that there is a natural aristocracy among
men. The grounds of this are virtue and talents. Formerly, bodily
powers gave place among the aristoi. But since the invention of gun-
powder has armed the weak as well as the strong with missile death,
bodily strength, like beauty, good humor, politeness and other accom-
plishments, has become but an auxiliary ground of distinction. There
is also an artificial aristocracy, founded on wealth and birth, without
either virtue or talents; for with these it would belong to the first
class. The natural aristocracy I consider as the most precious gift of
nature, for the instruction, the trusts, and government of society. And
indeed, it would have been inconsistent in creation to have formed man
for the social state, and not to have provided virtue and wisdom
enough to manage the concerns of the society. May we not even say,
that that form of government is the best, which provides the most
effectually for a pure selection of these natural aristoi into the offices
of government? The artificial aristocracy is a mischievous ingredient
in government, and provision should be made to prevent its ascend-
ency. . . .

With respect to aristocracy, we should further consider, that before
the establishment of the American States, nothing was known to history but the man of the old world, crowded within limits either small
or overcharged, and steeped in the vices which that situation generates.
A government adapted to such men would be one thing; but a very
different one, that for the man of these States. Here every one may
have land to labor for himself, if he chooses; or, preferring the exercise
of any other industry, may exact for it such compensation as not only
to afford a comfortable subsistence, but wherewith to provide for a

[3] Memorial Edition, XIII, 396–402.

cessation from labor in old age. Every one, by his property, or by his satisfactory situation, is interested in the support of law and order. And such men may safely and advantageously reserve to themselves a wholesome control over their public affairs, and a degree of freedom, which, in the hands of the *canaille* of the cities of Europe, would be instantly perverted to the demolition and destruction of everything public and private. The history of the last twenty-five years of France, and of the last forty years in America, nay of its last two hundred years, proves the truth of both parts of this observation.

But even in Europe a change has sensibly taken place in the mind of man. Science had liberated the ideas of those who read and reflect, and the American example had kindled feelings of right in the people. An insurrection has consequently begun, of science, talents, and courage against rank and birth, which have fallen into contempt. It has failed in its first effort, because the mobs of the cities, the instrument used for its accomplishment, debased by ignorance, poverty, and vice, could not be restrained to rational action. But the world will recover from the panic of this first catastrophe. Science is progressive, and talents and enterprise on the alert. Resort may be had to the people of the country, a more governable power from their principles and subordination; and rank, and birth and tinsel-aristocracy will finally shrink into insignificance, even there. This, however, we have no right to meddle with. It suffices for us, if the moral and physical condition of our own citizens qualifies them to select the able and good for the direction of their government, with a recurrence of elections at such short periods as will enable them to displace an unfaithful servant, before the mishief he meditates may be irremediable. . . .

"THE HOUR OF EMANCIPATION IS ADVANCING"[4]

To Edward Coles

Monticello, August 25th, '14

Dear Sir,—Your favour of July 31, was duly received, and was read with peculiar pleasure. The sentiments breathed through the whole do honor to both the head and heart of the writer. Mine on the subject of slavery of negroes have long since been in possession of the public, and time has only served to give them stronger root. The love of justice and the love of country plead equally the cause of these people, and it is a moral reproach to us that they should have pleaded

[4] Ford, IX, 477–78.

it so long in vain, and should have produced not a single effort, nay I fear not much serious willingness to relieve them & ourselves from our present condition of moral & political reprobation. From those of the former generation who were in the fulness of age when I came into public life, which was while our controversy with England was on paper only, I soon saw that nothing was to be hoped. Nursed and educated in the daily habit of seeing the degraded condition, both bodily and mental, of those unfortunate beings, not reflecting that that degradation was very much the work of themselves & their fathers, few minds have yet doubted but that they were as legitimate subjects of property as their horses and cattle. The quiet and monotonous course of colonial life has been disturbed by no alarm, and little reflection on the value of liberty. And when alarm was taken at an enterprize on their own, it was not easy to carry them to the whole length of the principles which they invoked for themselves. In the first or second session of the Legislature after I became a member, I drew to this subject the attention of Col. Bland, one of the oldest, ablest, & most respected members, and he undertook to move for certain moderate extensions on the protection of the laws to these people. I seconded his motion, and, as a younger member, was more spared in the debate; but he was denounced as an enemy of his country, & was treated with the grossest indecorum. From an early stage of our revolution other & more distant duties were assigned to me, so that from that time till my return from Europe in 1789, and I may say till I returned to reside at home in 1809, I had little opportunity of knowing the progress of public sentiment here on this subject. I had always hoped that the younger generation receiving their early impressions after the flame of liberty had been kindled in every breast, & had become as it were the vital spirit of every American that the generous temperament of youth, analogous to the motion of their blood, and above the suggestions of avarice, would have sympathized with oppression wherever found, and proved their love of liberty beyond their own share of it. But my intercourse with them, since my return has not been sufficient to ascertain that they had made towards this point the progress I had hoped. Your solitary but welcome voice is the first which has brought this sound to my ear; and I have considered the general silence which prevails on this subject as indicating an apathy unfavorable to every hope. Yet the hour of emancipation is advancing, in the march of time. . . .

ON MANUFACTURES [5]

To Benjamin Austin

Monticello, January 9, 1816

. . . Your opinions on the events which have taken place in France, are entirely just, so far as these events are yet developed. But they have not reached their ultimate termination. There is still an awful void between the present and what is to be the last chapter of that history; and I fear it is to be filled with abominations as frightful as those which have already disgraced it. That nation is too high-minded, has too much innate force, intelligence and elasticity, to remain under its present compression. Samson will arise in his strength, as of old, and as of old will burst asunder the withes and the cords, and the webs of the Philistines. But what are to be the scenes of havoc and horror, and how widely they may spread between brethren of the same house, our ignorance of the interior feuds and antipathies of the country places beyond our ken. It will end, nevertheless, in a representative government, in a government in which the will of the people will be a effective ingredient. This important element has taken root in the European mind, and will have its growth; their despots, sensible of this, are already offering this modification of their governments, as if of their own accord. Instead of the parricide treason of Bonaparte, in perverting the means confided to him as a republican magistrate, to the subversion of that republic and erection of a military despotism for himself and his family, had he used it honestly for the establishment and support of a free government in his own country, France would now have been in freedom and rest; and her example operating in a contrary direction, every nation in Europe would have had a goverment over which the will of the people would have had some control. His atrocious egotism has checked the salutary progress of principle, and deluged it with rivers of blood which are not yet run out. To the vast sum of devastation and of human misery, of which he has been the guilty cause, much is still to be added. But the object is fixed in the eye of nations, and they will press on to its accomplishment and to the general amelioration of the condition of man. What a germ have we planted, and how faithfully should we cherish the parent tree at home! You tell me I am quoted by those who wish to continue our depend-

[5] Ford, X, 7–11.

ence on England for manufactures. There was a time when I might have been so quoted with more candor, but within the thirty years which have since elapsed, how are circumstances changed! We were then in peace. Our independent place among nations was acknowledged. A commerce which offered the raw material in exchange for the same material after receiving the last touch of industry, was worthy of welcome to all nations. It was expected that those especially to whom manufacturing industry was important, would cherish the friendship of such customers by every favor, by every inducement, and particularly cultivate their peace by every act of justice and friendship. Under this prospect the question seemed legitimate, whether, with such an immensity of unimproved land, courting the hand of husbandry, the industry of agriculture, or that of manufactures, would add most to the national wealth? And the doubt was entertained on this consideration chiefly, that to the labor of the husbandman a vast addition is made by the spontaneous energies of the earth on which it is employed: for one grain of wheat committed to the earth, she renders twenty, thirty, and even fifty fold, whereas to the labor of the manufacturer nothing is added. Pounds of flax, in his hands, yield, on the contrary, but pennyweights of lace. This exchange, too, laborious as it might seem, what a field did it promise for the occupations of the ocean; what a nursery for that class of citizens who were to exercise and maintain our equal rights on that element? This was the state of things in 1785, when the "Notes on Virginia" were first printed; when, the ocean being open to all nations, and their common right in it acknowledged and exercised under regulations sanctioned by the assent and usage of all, it was thought that the doubt might claim some consideration. But who in 1785 could foresee the rapid depravity which was to render the close of that century the disgrace of the history of man? Who could have imagined that the two most distinguished in the rank of nations, for science and civilization, would have suddenly descended from that honorable eminence, and setting at defiance all those moral laws established by the Author of nature between nation and nation, as between man and man, would cover earth and sea with robberies and piracies, merely because strong enough to do it with temporal impunity; and that under this disbandment of nations from social order, we should have been despoiled of a thousand ships, and have thousands of our citizens reduced to Algerine slavery. Yet all this has taken place. One of these nations interdicted to our vessels all harbors of the globe without having first proceeded to some one of hers, there paid a tribute proportioned to the cargo, and obtained her license to proceed to the port of destination. The other declared them to be lawful prize if they had touched at the port, or been visited by a ship of the enemy nation. Thus were we completely excluded from the ocean. Compare this state of things with that of '85, and say whether an opinion founded in the circumstances of that day can be fairly applied to those of the present. We have experienced what we did not then believe, that there exists both profligacy and power enough to exclude us from the field of interchange with other nations: that to be independent for the comforts of life we must fabricate them ourselves. We must now place the manufacturer by the side of the agriculturist. The former question is suppressed, or rather assumes a new form. Shall we make our own comforts, or go without them, at the will of a foreign nation? He, therefore, who is now against domestic manufacture, must be for reducing us either to dependence on that foreign nation, or to be clothed in skins, and to live like wild beasts in dens and caverns. I am not one of these; experience has taught me that manufactures are now as necessary to our independence as to our comfort; and if those who quote me as of a different opinion, will keep pace with me in purchasing nothing foreign where an equivalent of domestic fabric can be obtained, without regard to difference of price, it will not be our fault if we do not soon have a supply at home equal to our demand, and wrest that weapon of distress from the hand which has wielded it. If it shall be proposed to go beyond our own supply, the question of '85 will then recur, will our *surplus* labor be then most beneficially employed in the culture of the earth, or in the fabrications of art? We have time yet for consideration, before that question will press upon us; and the maxim to be applied will depend on the circumstances which shall then exist; for in so complicated a science as political economy, no one axiom can be laid down as wise and expedient for all times and circumstances, and for their contraries. Inattention to this is what has called for this explanation, which reflection would have rendered unnecessary with the candid, while nothing will do it with those who use the former opinion only as a stalking horse, to cover their disloyal propensities to keep us in eternal vassalage to a foreign and unfriendly people.

I salute you with assurances of great respect and esteem.

THE MISSOURI QUESTION [6]

To John Holmes

Monticello, April 22, 1820

I thank you, dear Sir, for the copy you have been so kind as to send me of the letter to your constituents on the Missouri question. It is a perfect justification to them. I had for a long time ceased to read newspapers, or pay any attention to public affairs, confident they were in good hands, and content to be a passenger in our bark to the shore from which I am not distant. But this momentous question, like a fire-bell in the night, awakened and filled me with terror. I considered it at once as the knell of the Union. It is hushed, indeed, for the moment. But this is a reprieve only, not a final sentence. A geographical line, coinciding with a marked principle, moral and political, once conceived and held up to the angry passions of men, will never be obliterated; and every new irritation will mark it deeper and deeper. I can say, with conscious truth, that there is not a man on earth who would sacrifice more than I would to relieve us from this heavy reproach, in any *practicable* way. The cession of that kind of property, for so it is misnamed, is a bagatelle which would not cost me a second thought, if, in that way, a general emancipation and *expatriation* could be effected; and, gradually, and with due sacrifices, I think it might be. But as it is, we have the wolf by the ears, and we can neither hold him, nor safely let him go. Justice is in one scale, and self-preservation in the other. Of one thing I am certain, that as the passage of slaves from one State to another, would not make a slave of a single human being who would not be so without it, so their diffusion over a greater surface would make them individually happier, and proportionally facilitate the accomplishment of their emancipation, by dividing the burden on a greater number of coadjutors. An abstinence too, from this act of power, would remove the jealousy excited by the undertaking of Congress to regulate the condition of the different descriptions of men composing a State. This certainly is the exclusive right of every State which nothing in the Constitution has taken from them and given to the General Government. Could Congress, for example, say, that the non-freemen of Connecticut shall be freemen, or that they shall not emigrate into any other State?

[6] Memorial Edition, XV, 248–50.

I regret that I am now to die in the belief, that the useless sacrifice of themselves by the generation of 1776, to acquire self-government and happiness to their country, is to be thrown away by the unwise and unworthy passions of their sons, and that my only consolation is to be, that I live not to weep over it. If they would but dispassionately weigh the blessings they will throw away, against an abstract principle more likely to be effected by union than by scission, they would pause before they would perpetrate this act of suicide on themselves, and of treason against the hopes of the world. To yourself, as the faithful advocate of the Union, I tender the offering of my high esteem and respect.

"TAKE CARE OF ME WHEN DEAD"[7]

To James Madison

Monticello, February 17, 1826

. . . In the selection of our Law Professor, we must be rigorously attentive to his political principles. You will recollect that before the Revolution, Coke Littleton was the universal elementary book of law students, and a sounder Whig never wrote, nor of profounder learning in the orthodox doctrines of the British constitution, or in what were called English liberties. You remember also that our lawyers were then all Whigs. But when his black-letter text, and uncouth but cunning learning got out of fashion, and the honeyed Mansfieldism of Blackstone became the students' hornbook, from that moment, that profession (the nursery of our Congress) began to slide into toryism, and nearly all the young brood of lawyers now are of that hue. They suppose themselves, indeed, to be Whigs, because they no longer know what Whigism or republicanism means. It is in our seminary that that vestal flame is to be kept alive; it is thence it is to spread anew over our own and the sister States. If we are true and vigilant in our trust, within a dozen or twenty years a majority of our own legislature will be from one school, and many disciples will have carried its doctrines home with them to their several States, and will have leavened thus the whole mass. . . .

You will have seen in the newspapers some proceedings in the legislature, which have cost me much mortification. My own debts had become considerable, but not beyond the effect of some lopping of prop-

[7] Memorial Edition, XVI, 156–59.

erty, which would have been little felt, when our friend Nicholas gave me the *coup de grace*. Ever since that I have been paying twelve hundred dollars a year interest on his debt, which, with my own, was absorbing so much of my annual income, as that the maintenance of my family was making deep and rapid inroads on my capital, and had already done it. Still, sales at a fair price would leave me completely provided. Had crops and prices for several years been such as to maintain a steady competition of substantial bidders at market, all would have been safe. But the long succession of years of stunted crops, of reduced prices, the general prostration of the farming business, under levies for the support of manufacturers, etc., with the calamitous fluctuations of value in our paper medium, have kept agriculture in a state of abject depression. . . .

Reflecting on these things, the practice occurred to me, of selling, on fair valuation, and by way of lottery, often resorted to before the Revolution to effect large sales, and still in constant usage in every State for individual as well as corporation purposes. If it is permitted in my case, my lands here alone, with the mills, etc., will pay everything, and leave me Monticello and a farm free. If refused, I must sell everything here, perhaps considerably in Bedford, move thither with my family, where I have not even a log hut to put my head into, and whether ground for burial, will depend on the depredations which, under the form of sales, shall have been committed on my property. The question then with me was *ultrum horum?* But why afflict you with these details? Indeed, I cannot tell, unless pains are lessened by communication with a friend. The friendship which has subsisted between us, now half a century, and the harmony of our political principles and pursuits, have been sources of constant happiness to me through that long period. And if I remove beyond the reach of attentions to the University, or beyond the bourne of life itself, as I soon must, it is a comfort to leave that institution under your care, and an assurance that it will not be wanting. It has also been a great solace to me, to believe that you are engaged in vindicating to posterity the course we have pursued for preserving to them, in all their purity, the blessings of self-government, which we had assisted too in acquiring for them. If ever the earth has beheld a system of administration conducted with a single and steadfast eye to the general interest and happiness of those committed to it, one which, protected by truth, can never know reproach, it is that to which our lives have been devoted. To myself you have been a pillar of support through life. Take care of me when dead, and be assured that I shall leave with you my last affections.

THE RIGHTS OF MAN [8]

To Roger C. Weightman

Monticello, June 24. 1826

Respected Sir,—The kind invitation I receive from you, on the part of the citizens of the city of Washington, to be present with them at their celebration on the fiftieth anniversary of American Independence, as one of the surviving signers of an instrument pregnant with our own, and the fate of the world, is most flattering to myself, and heightened by the honorable accompaniment proposed for the comfort of such a journey. It adds sensibly to the sufferings of sickness, to be deprived by it of a personal participation in the rejoicings of that day. But acquiescence is a duty, under circumstances not placed among those we are permitted to control. I should, indeed, with peculiar delight, have met and exchanged there congratulations personally with the small band, the remnant of that host of worthies, who jointed with us on that day, in the bold and doubtful election we were to make for our country, beween submission or the sword; and to have enjoyed with them the consolatory fact, that our fellow citizens, after half a century of experience and prosperity, continue to approve the choice we made. May it be to the world, what I believe it will be (to some parts sooner, to others later, but finally to all), the signal of arousing men to burst the chains under which monkish ignorance and superstition had persuaded them to bind themselves, and to assume the blessings and security of self-government. That form which we have substituted, restores the free right to the unbounded exercise of reason and freedom of opinion. All eyes are opened, or opening, to the rights of man. The general spread of the light of science has already laid open to every view the palpable truth, that the mass of mankind has not been born with saddles on their backs, nor a favored few booted and spurred, ready to ride them legitimately, by the grace of God. These are grounds of hope for others. For ourselves, let the annual return of this day forever refresh our recollections of these rights, and an undiminished devotion to them. . . .

[8] Memorial Edition, XVI, 181–82.

JEFFERSON SUMS UP [9]

February, 1826

. . . I came of age in 1764, and was soon put into the nomination of justice of the county in which I live, and at the first election following I became one of its representatives in the Legislature.

I was thence sent to the old Congress.

Then employed two years with Mr. Pendleton and Mr. Wythe on the revisal and reduction to a single code of the whole body of the British statutes, the acts of our Assembly, and certain parts of the common law.

Then elected Governor.

Next to the Legislature, and to Congress again.

Sent to Europe as Minister Plenipotentiary.

Appointed Secretary of State to the new government.

Elected Vice-President, and

President.

And lastly, a Visitor and Rector of the University.

In these different offices, with scarcely any interval between them, I have been in the public service now sixty-one years; and during the far greater part of the time, in foreign countries or in other States. Every one knows how inevitably a Virginia estate goes to ruin, when the owner is so far distant as to be unable to pay attention to it himself; and the more especially, when the line of his employment is of a character to abstract and alienate his mind entirely from the knowledge necessary to good, and even to saving management.

If it were thought worth while to specify any particular services rendered, I would refer to the specification of them made by the Legislature itself in their Farewell Address, on my retiring from the Presidency, February, 1809. There is one, however, not therein specified, the most important in its consequences, of any transaction in any portion of my life; to wit, the head I personally made against the federal principles and proceedings, during the administration of Mr. Adams. Their usurpations and violations of the constitution at that period, and their majority in both Houses of Congress, were so great, so decided, and so daring, that after combating their aggressions, inch by inch, without being able in the least to check their career, the republican leaders thought it would be best for them to give up their useless efforts there, go home, get into their respective Legislatures, em-

[9] Ford, X, 365–72.

body whatever of resistance they could be formed into, and if ineffectual, to perish there as in the last ditch. All, therefore, retired. leaving Mr. Gallatin alone in the House of Representatives, and myself in the Senate, where I then presided as Vice-President. Remaining at our posts, and bidding defiance to the brow beatings and insults by which they endeavored to drive us off also, we kept the mass of republicans in phalanx together, until the Legislatures could be brought up to the charge; and nothing on earth is more certain, than that if myself particularly, placed by my office of Vice-President at the head of the republicans, had given way and withdrawn from my post, the republicans throughout the Union would have given up in despair, and the cause would have been lost forever. By holding on, we obtained time for the Legislatures to come up with their weight; and those of Virginia and Kentucky particularly, but more especially the former, by their celebrated resolutions, saved the constitution at its last gasp. No person who was not a witness of the scenes of that gloomy period, can form any idea of the afflicting persecutions and personal indignities we had to brook. They saved our country however. The spirits of the people were so much subdued and reduced to despair by the X Y Z imposture, and other stratagems and machinations, that they would have sunk into apathy and monarchy, as the only form of government which could maintain itself.

If Legislative services are worth mentioning, and the stamp of liberality and equality, which was necessary to be imposed on our laws in the first crisis of our birth as a nation, was of any value, they will find that the leading and most important laws of that day were prepared by myself, and carried chiefly by my efforts; supported, indeed, by able and faithful coadjutors from the ranks of the House, very effective as seconds, but who would not have taken the field as leaders.

The prohibition of the further importation of slaves was the first of these measures in time.

This was followed by the abolition of entails, which broke up the hereditary and high-handed aristocracy, which, by accumulating immense masses of property in single lines of families, had divided our country into two distinct orders, of nobles and plebeians.

But further to complete the equality among our citizens so essential to the maintenance of republican government, it was necessary to abolish the principle of primogeniture. I drew the law of descents, giving equal inheritance to sons and daughters, which made a part of the revised code.

The attack on the establishment of a dominant religion, was first made by myself. It could be carried at first only by a suspension of salaries for one year, by battling it again at the next session for another year, and so from year to year, until the public mind was ripened for the bill for establishing religious freedom, which I had prepared for the revised code also. This was at length established permanently, and by the efforts chiefly of Mr. Madison, being myself in Europe at the time that work was brought forward.

To these particular services, I think I might add the establishment of our University, as principally my work, acknowledging at the same time, as I do, the great assistance received from my able colleagues of the Visitation. But my residence in the vicinity threw, of course, on me the chief burthen of the enterprise, as well of the buildings as of the general organization and care of the whole. The effect of this institution on the future fame, fortune and prosperity of our country, can as yet be seen but at a distance. But an hundred well-educated youths, which it will turn out annually, and ere long, will fill all its offices with men of superior qualifications, and raise it from its humble state to an eminence among its associates which it has never yet known; no, not in its brightest days. That institution is now qualified to raise its youth to an order of science unequalled in any other State; and this superiority will be the greater from the free range of mind encouraged there, and the restraint imposed at other seminaries by the shackles of a domineering hierarchy, and a bigoted adhesion to ancient habits. Those now on the theatre of affairs will enjoy the ineffable happiness of seeing themselves succeeded by sons of a grade of science beyond their own ken. Our sister States will also be repairing to the same fountains of instruction, will bring hither their genius to be kindled at our fire, and will carry back the fraternal affections which, nourished by the same *alma mater,* will knit us to them by the indissoluble bonds of early personal friendships. The good Old Dominion, the blessed mother of us all, will then raise her head with pride among the nations, will present to them that splendor of genius which she has ever possessed, but has too long suffered to rest uncultivated and unknown, and will become a centre of ralliance to the States whose youth she has instructed, and, as it were, adopted.

I claim some share in the merits of this great work of regeneration. My whole labors, now for many years, have been devoted to it, and I stand pledged to follow it up through the remnant of life remaining to me. . . .

EPITAPH [10]

> Could the dead feel any interest in Monu-
> ments or other remembrances of them. . .
> the following would be to my Manes the most
> gratifying.
> On the grave
>   a plain die or cube of 3 f. without any
> mouldings, surmounted by an Obelisk of
> 6 f. height, each of a single stone:
> on the faces of the Obelisk the following
> inscription, & not a word more
>   'Here was buried
>   Thomas Jefferson
> Author of the Declaration of American Independence
>   of the Statute of Virginia for religious freedom
>   & Father of the University of Virginia.'
> because by these, as testimonials that I have lived, I
> wish most to be remembered.

[10] Memorial Edition, I, Facsimile facing p. 262.

HIS WORLD LOOKS AT JEFFERSON

Jefferson has come to be recognized as a versatile genius, not easy to depict if one would do justice to his mind and personality. Henry Adams, who had an inherited and temperamental bias against him, nonetheless truly wrote that while other American statesmen could be treated in a parenthesis, Jefferson "could be painted only touch by touch, with a fine pencil, and the perfection of the likeness depended upon the shifting and uncertain flicker of its semi-transparent shadows."

While the ideal portrait still awaits its maker, something at least of the likeness may be seen in this series of views written about Jefferson by his own contemporaries. Glimpses of the private man at home at Monticello, informal views of the official man, and brief character appraisals by his great opponents— Adams, Hamilton, and Marshall—and his greatest friend and close collaborator, James Madison, provide invaluable suggestions for a portrait. These selections are further supplemented by appreciative sketches of the whole man viewed in retrospect by men who knew him and who wrote upon the occasion of Jefferson's death or some years thereafter.

8

Visits with Jefferson at Monticello

The Declaration of Independence made Jefferson a world-famous figure, even though he was but thirty-three years of age when he penned the immortal document. From that time until the very last weeks of his life, Jefferson extended the courtesies of a Virginia gentleman-host to a steady stream of visitors from home and abroad. Many of them were moved to record their impressions of the man and the home he lavished with lifelong attention. The selections below attempt to indicate something of the range of these visitors over time and from different countries. The first two are by noted Frenchmen, one by the Marquis de Chastellux in 1782 before Jefferson went abroad, and the other by the Duc de La Rochefoucauld-Liancourt in 1796 after Jefferson had been in France as American Minister and had served in Washington's Cabinet as the first Secretary of State. The third selection is by George Ticknor, a brilliant young Bostonian, who visited Jefferson in 1815 when the ex-President was already deeply interested in developing his plans for a great new university. The fourth selection reports the visit of an English traveler who saw Jefferson in 1817. The final selection provides comments by a titled German visitor on the aged Jefferson, the year before he died.

THE MARQUIS DE CHASTELLUX—1782[1]

. . . The conversation continued and brought us insensibly to the foot of the mountains. On the summit of one of them we discovered the house of Mr. Jefferson, which stands preeminent in these retirements; it was himself who built it and preferred this situation; for although he possessed considerable property in the neighborhood, there was nothing to prevent him from fixing his residence wherever he thought proper. But it was a debt nature owed to a philosopher and a man of taste, that in his own possessions he should find a spot where he might best study and enjoy her. He calls his house Monticello (in Italian, Little Mountain,) a very modest title, for it is situated upon a very lofty one, but which announces the owner's attachment to the language of Italy; and above all to the fine arts, of which that country was the cradle, and is still the asylum. As I had no farther occasion for a guide, I separated from the Irishman; and after ascending by a tolerably commodious road, for more than half an hour, we arrived at Monticello. This house, of which Mr. Jefferson was the architect, and often one of the workmen, is rather elegant, and in the Italian taste, though not without fault; it consists of one large square pavillion, the entrance of which is by two porticos ornamented with pillars. The ground floor consists chiefly of a very large lofty saloon, which is to be decorated entirely in the antique style: above it is a library of the same form, two small wings, with only a ground floor, and attic story,

---

[1] *Travels in North-America in the Years 1780–81–82* (New York, 1827), pp. 81–82.

are joined to this pavillion, and communicate with the kitchen, offices, &c. which will form a kind of basement story over which runs a terrace. My object in this short description is only to show the difference between this, and the other houses of the country; for we may safely aver, that Mr. Jefferson is the first American who has consulted the fine arts to know how he should shelter himself from the weather. But it is on himself alone I ought to bestow my time. Let me describe to you a man, not yet forty, tall, and with a mild and pleasing countenance, but whose mind and understanding are ample substitutes for every exterior grace. An American, who without ever having quitted his own country, is at once a musician, skilled in drawing, a geometrician, an astronomer, a natural philosopher, legislator, and statesman. A senator of America, who sat for two years in that famous Congress which brought about the revolution; and which is never mentioned without respect, though unhappily not without regret: a governor of Virginia, who filled this difficult station during the invasions of Arnold, of Phillips, and of Cornwallis; a philosopher, in voluntary retirement from the world, and public business, because he loves the world, inasmuch only as he can flatter himself with being useful to mankind; and the minds of his countrymen are not yet in a condition either to bear the light, or to suffer contradiction. A mild and amiable wife, charming children, of whose education he himself takes charge, a house to embellish, great provisions to improve, and the arts and sciences to cultivate; these are what remain to Mr. Jefferson, after having played a principal character on the theatre of the new world, and which he preferred to the honourable commission of Minister Plenipotentiary in Europe. The visit which I made him was not unexpected, for he had long since invited me to come and pass a few days with him, in the centre of the mountains; notwithstanding which I found his first appearance serious, nay even cold; but before I had been two hours with him we were as intimate as if we had passed our whole lives together; walking, books, but above all, a conversation always varied and interesting, always supported by that sweet satisfaction experienced by two persons, who in communicating their sentiments and opinions, are invariably in unison, and who understand each other at the first hint, made four days pass away like so many minutes.

THE DUC DE LA ROCHEFOUCAULD–LIANCOURT—1796[2]

Monticello is situated four miles from Milford, in that chain of mountains which stretches from James-River to the Rappahannock, twenty-eight miles in front of the Blue-Ridge, and in a direction parallel to those mountains. This chain, which runs uninterrupted in its small extent, assumes successively the names of the West, South, and Green Mountains.

It is in the part known by the name of the South-Mountains that Monticello is situated. The house stands on the summit of the mountain, and the taste and arts of Europe have been consulted in the formation of its plan. Mr. Jefferson had commenced its construction before the American Revolution; since that epocha his life has been constantly engaged in public affairs, and he has not been able to complete the execution of the whole extent of the project which it seems he had at first conceived. That part of the building which was finished has suffered from the suspension of the work, and Mr. Jefferson, who two years since resumed the habits and leisure of private life, is now employed in repairing the damage occasioned by this interruption, and still more by his absence; he continues his original plan, and even improves on it, by giving to his buildings more elevation and extent. He intends that they should consist only of one story, crowned with balustrades; and a dome is to be constructed in the center of the structure. The apartments will be large and convenient; the decoration, both outside and inside, simple, yet regular and elegant. Monticello, according to its first plan, was infinitely superior to all other houses in America, in point of taste and convenience; but at that time Mr. Jefferson had studied taste and the fine arts in books only. His travels in Europe have supplied him with models; he has appropriated them to his design; and his new plan, the execution of which is already much advanced, will be accomplished before the end of next year, and then his house will certainly deserve to be ranked with the most pleasant mansions in France and England.

Mr. Jefferson's house commands one of the most extensive prospects you can meet with. . . . On this mountain, and in the surrounding valleys, on both banks of the Rivanna, are situated the five thousand

[2] From *Travels Through the United States of North America, the Country of the Iroquois, and Upper Canada, in the Years, 1795, 1796, and 1797* (London, 1800). Cited in Sarah N. Randolph, *The Domestic Life of Thomas Jefferson* (New York: Harper and Brothers, 1871), pp. 235–38.

acres of land which Mr. Jefferson possesses in this part of Virginia. Eleven hundred and twenty only are cultivated. The land left to the care of stewards has suffered as well as the buildings from the long absence of the master; according to the custom of the country it has been exhausted by successive culture. Its situation on declivities of hills and mountains renders a careful cultivation more necessary than is requisite in lands situated in a flat and even country; the common routine is more pernicious, and more judgement and mature thought are required than in a different soil. This forms at present the chief employment of Mr. Jefferson. . . .

In private life Mr. Jefferson displays a mild, easy and obliging temper, though he is somewhat cold and reserved. His conversation is of the most agreeable kind, and he possesses a stock of information not inferior to that of any other man. In Europe he would hold a distinguished rank among men of letters, and as such he has already appeared there; at present he is employed with activity and perseverance in the management of his farms and buildings; and he orders, directs, and pursues in the minutest detail every branch of business relative to them. I found him in the midst of the harvest, from which the scorching heat of the sun does not prevent his attendance. His negroes are nourished, clothed, and treated as well as white servants could be. As he cannot expect any assistance from the two small neighbouring towns, every article is made on his farm; his negroes are cabinet-makers, carpenters, masons, bricklayers, smiths, &c. The children he employs in a nail-manufactory, which yields already a considerable profit. The young and old negresses spin for the clothing of the rest. He animates them by rewards and distinctions; in fine, his superior mind directs the management of his domestic concerns with the same abilities, activity, and regularity, which he evinced in the conduct of public affairs, and which he is calculated to display in every situation of life. . . .

GEORGE TICKNOR—1815[3]

We left Charlottesville on Saturday morning, the 4th of February, for Mr. Jefferson's. He lives, you know, on a mountain, which he has named Monticello, and which, perhaps you do not know, is a synonyme for Carter's mountain. The ascent of this steep, savage hill, was as pensive and slow as Satan's ascent to Paradise. We were obliged to wind two thirds round its sides before we reached the artificial lawn

[3] From *Life, Letters, and Journals of George Ticknor*, I (Boston, 1880), 34–35.

on which the house stands; and when we had arrived there, we were
about six hundred feet, I understand, above the stream which flows
at its foot. It is an abrupt mountain. The fine growth of ancient forest-
trees conceals its sides and shades part of its summit. The prospect is
admirable. . . . The lawn on the top, as I hinted, was artificially
formed by cutting down the peak of the height. In its centre, and
facing the southeast, Mr. Jefferson has placed his house, which is of
brick, two stories high in the wings, with a piazza in front of a receding
centre. It is built, I suppose, in the French style. You enter, by a glass
folding-door, into a hall which reminds you of Fielding's "Man of the
Mountain," by the strange furniture of its walls. On one side hang the
head and horns of an elk, a deer, and a buffalo; another is covered
with curiosities which Lewis and Clarke found in their wild and peril-
ous expedition. On the third, among many other striking matters, was
the head of a mammoth, or, as Cuvier calls it, a mastadon, containing
the only *os frontis,* Mr. Jefferson tells me, that has yet been found. On
the fourth side, in odd union with a fine painting of the Repentance
of Saint Peter, is an Indian map on leather, of the southern waters of
the Missouri, and an Indian representation of a bloody battle, handed
down in their traditions.

Through this hall—or rather museum—we passed to the dining-
room, and sent our letters to Mr. Jefferson, who was of course in his
study. Here again we found ourselves surrounded with paintings that
seemed good.

We had hardly time to glance at the pictures before Mr. Jefferson
entered; and if I was astonished to find Mr. Madison short and somewhat awkward, I was doubly astonished to find Mr. Jefferson, whom
I had always supposed to be a small man, more than six feet high,
with dignity in his appearance, and ease and graciousness in his
manners. . . . He rang, and sent to Charlottesville for our baggage,
and, as dinner approached, took us to the drawing-room,—a large and
rather elegant room, twenty or thirty feet high,—which, with the hall
I have described, composed the whole centre of the house, from top
to bottom. The floor of this room is tessellated. It is formed of alternate
diamonds of cherry and beech, and kept polished as highly as if it
were of fine mahogany.

Here are the best pictures of the collection. Over the fireplace is
the Laughing and Weeping Philosophers, dividing the world between
them; on its right, the earliest navigators to America,—Columbus,
Americus Vespuccius, Magellan, etc.,—copied, Mr. Jefferson said, from
originals in the Florence Gallery. Farther round, Mr. Madison in the
plain, Quaker-like dress of his youth, Lafayette in his Revolutionary

uniform, and Franklin in the dress in which we always see him. There were other pictures, and a copy of Raphael's Transfiguration.

We conversed on various subjects until dinner-time, and at dinner were introduced to the grown members of his family. These are his only remaining child, Mrs. Randolph, her husband, Colonel Randolph, and the two oldest of their unmarried children, Thomas Jefferson and Ellen; and I assure you I have seldom met a pleasanter party.

The evening passed away pleasantly in general conversation, of which Mr. Jefferson was necessarily the leader. I shall probably surprise you by saying that, in conversation, he reminded me of Dr. Freeman. He has the same discursive manner and love of paradox, with the same appearance of sobriety and cool reason. He seems equally fond of American antiquities, and especially the antiquities of his native State, and talks of them with freedom and, I suppose, accuracy. He has, too, the appearance of that fairness and simplicity which Dr. Freeman has; and, if the parallel holds no further here, they will again meet on the ground of their love of old books and young society.

On Sunday morning, after breakfast, Mr. Jefferson asked me into his library, and there I spent the forenoon of that day as I had that of yesterday. This collection of books, now so much talked about, consists of about seven thousand volumes, contained in a suite of fine rooms, and is arranged in the catalogue, and on the shelves, according to the divisions and subdivisions of human learning by Lord Bacon. In so short a time I could not, of course, estimate its value, even if I had been competent to do so.

Perhaps the most curious single specimen—or, at least, the most characteristic of the man and expressive of his hatred of royalty—was a collection which he had bound up in six volumes, and lettered "The Book of Kings," consisting of the "Memoires de la Princesse de Bareith," two volumes; "Les Memoires de la Comtesse de la Motte," two volumes; the "Trial of the Duke of York," one volume; and *"The Book,"* one volume. These documents of regal scandal seemed to be favorites with the philosopher, who pointed them out to me with a satisfaction somewhat inconsistent with the measured gravity he claims in relation to such subjects generally. . . .

There is a breathing of notional philosophy in Mr. Jefferson,—in his dress, his house, his conversation. His setness, for instance, in wearing very sharp toed shoes, corduroy small-clothes, and red plush waistcoat, which have been laughed at till he might perhaps wisely have dismissed them.

So, though he told me he thought Charron, "De la Sagesse," the best treatise on moral philosophy ever written, and an obscure Review of Montesquieu, by Dupont de Nemours, the best political work that had been printed for fifty years,—though he talked very freely of the natural impossibility that one generation should bind another to pay a public debt, and of the expediency of vesting all the legislative authority of a State in one branch, and the executive authority in another, and leaving them to govern it by joint discretion,—I considered such opinions simply as curious *indicia* of an extraordinary character.

FRANCIS HALL—1817[4]

Having an introduction to Mr. Jefferson, I ascended his *little mountain* on a fine morning, which gave the situation its due effect. The whole of the sides and base are covered with forest, through which roads have been cut circularly, so that the winding may be shortened or prolonged at pleasure: the summit is an open lawn, near to the south side of which, the house is built, with its garden just descending the brow: the saloon, or central hall, is ornamented with several pieces of antique sculpture, Indian arms, Mammoth bones, and other curiosities collected from various parts of the Union. I found Mr. Jefferson tall in person, but stooping and lean with old age; thus exhibiting that fortunate mode of bodily decay, which strips the frame of its most cumbersome parts, leaving it still strength of muscle and activity of limb: his deportment was exactly such as the Marquis de Chastellux describes it, above thirty years ago: "At first serious, nay even cold," but in a very short time relaxing into a most agreeable amenity; with an unabated flow of conversation on the most interesting topics, discust in the most gentlemanly, and philosophical manner. I walked with him round his grounds, to visit his pet trees, and improvements of various kinds. . . .

I slept a night at Monticello, and left it in the morning, with such a feeling as the traveller quits the mouldering remains of a Grecian temple, or the pilgrim a fountain in the desert. It would indeed argue great torpor, both of understanding and heart, to have looked without veneration and interest, on the man who drew up the declaration of American independence; who shared in the councils by which her freedom was established; whom the unbought voice of his fellow-citizens called to the exercise of a dignity, from which his own modera-

⁴ From *Travels in Canada, and the United States, in 1816 and 1817* (London, 1819). Cited in Sarah N. Randolph, *The Domestic Life of Thomas Jefferson* (New York: Harper and Brothers, 1871), pp. 365–68.

tion impelled him, when such example was most salutary, to withdraw; and who, while he dedicates the evening of his glorious days to the pursuits of science and literature, shuns none of the humbler duties of private life; but, having filled a seat higher than that of kings, succeeds with graceful dignity to that of the good neighbour, and becomes the friendly adviser, lawyer, physician, and even gardener of his vicinity. This is the "still small voice" of philosophy, deeper and holier than the lightnings and earthquakes which have preceded it. What monarch would venture thus to exhibit himself in the nakedness of his humanity? On what royal brow would the laurel replace the diadem? But they who are born and educated to be kings, are not expected to be philosophers.—That is a just answer, though no great compliment either to the governors or the governed.

DUKE OF SAXE–WEIMAR EISENACH—1825[5]

President Jefferson invited us to a family dinner; but as in Charlotteville there is but a single hackney-coach, and this being absent, we were obliged to go the three miles to Monticello on foot. . . .

The unsuccessful waiting for a carriage, and our long walk, caused such a delay, that we found the company at table when we entered; but Mr. Jefferson came very kindly to meet us, forced us to take our seats, and ordered dinner to be served up anew. He was an old man of eighty-six years of age, of tall stature, plain appearance, and long white hair.

In conversation he was very lively, and his spirits, as also his hearing and sight, seemed not to have decreased at all with his advancing age. I found in him a man who retained his faculties remarkably well in his old age, and one would have taken him for a man of sixty. He asked me what I had seen in Virginia. I eulogized all the places, that I was certain would meet with his approbation, and he seemed very much pleased. The company at the table, consisted of the family of his daughter, Mrs. Randolph, and of that of the professor of mathematics at the university, an Englishman, and of his wife. I turned the conversation to the subject of the university, and observed, that this was the favourite topic with Mr. Jefferson; he entertained very sanguine hopes as to the flourishing state of the university in future, and believed that it, and the Harvard University near Boston, would in a very short time be the only institutions, where the youth of the United

[5] From *Travels Through North America During the Years 1805 and 1826* (Philadelphia, 1828).

States would receive a truly classical and solid education. After dinner we intended to take our leave, in order to return to Charlotteville; but Mr. Jefferson would not consent to it. He pressed us to remain for the night at his house. The evening was spent by the fire; a great deal was said about travels, and objects of natural history; the fine arts were also introduced, of which Mr. Jefferson was a great admirer. He spoke also of his travels in France, and the country on the Rhine, where he was very much pleased. His description of Virginia is the best proof what an admirer he is of beauties of nature. He told us that it was only eight months since he could not ride on horseback; otherwise, he rode every day to visit the surrounding country; he entertained, however, hopes of being able to re-commence the next spring his favourite exercise. Between nine and ten o'clock in the evening, the company broke up, and a handsome room was assigned to me.

The next morning I took a walk round the house, and admired the beautiful panorama, which this spot presents. On the left, I saw the Blue Ridge, and between them and Monticello are smaller hills. Charlotteville and the University lay at my feet; before me, the valley of the Rivanna river, which farther on, makes its junction with the James river, and on my right was the flat part of Virginia, the extent of which is lost in distance; behind me was a towering hill, which limited the sight. The interior of the house was plain, and the furniture somewhat of an old fashion. In the entrance was a marble stove with Mr. Jefferson's bust, by Ceracchi. In the rooms hung several copies of the celebrated pictures of the Italian school, views of Monticello, Mount-Vernon, the principal buildings in Washington and Harper's Ferry; there were also an oil painting, and an engraving of the Natural Bridge, views of Niagara by Vanderlin, a sketch of the large picture by Trumbull, representing the surrender at Yorktown, and a pen drawing of Hector's departure, by Benjamin West, presented by him to General Kosciuszko; finally, several portraits of Mr. Jefferson, among which the best was that in profile by Stuart. In the saloon there were two busts, one of Napoleon as first consul, and another of the Emperor Alexander. Mr. Jefferson admired Napoleon's military talents, but did not love him. After breakfast, which we took with the family, we bid the respectable old man farewell, and set out upon our return on foot to Charlotteville.

Mr. Jefferson tendered us the use of his carriage, but I declined, as I preferred walking in a fine and cool morning. . . .

9
Informal Views of Jefferson in Office

JEFFERSON'S FIRST APPEARANCE AS SECRETARY OF STATE BEFORE A SENATE COMMITTEE—WILLIAM MACLAY—1790[1]

May 24th. . . . We had an appointment with Jefferson the Secretary of State at 6 O'Clock. When I came to the Hall Jefferson and the rest of the Committee were there. Jefferson is a slender Man. Has rather the Air of Stiffness in his Manner. His cloaths seem too small for him. He sits in a lounging Manner on one hip, commonly, and with one of his shoulders elevated much above the other. His face has a scrany Aspect. His whole figure has a loose shackling Air. He had a rambling Vacant look and nothing of that firm collected deportment which I expected would dignify the presence of a Secretary or Minister. I looked for Gravity, but a laxity of Manner, seemd shed about him. He spoke almost without ceasing. But even his discourse partook of his personal demeanor. It was loose and rambling and yet he scattered information wherever he went, and some even brilliant Sentiments sparkled from him. The information which he gave us respecting foreign Ministers &ca. was all high Spiced. He has been long enough abroad to catch the tone of European folly. He gave us a sentiment which seemd to savor rather of quaintness. "It is better to take the highest of the lowest, than the lowest of the highest." Translation: it is better to appoint a Chargé des Affaires with an handsome Salary, than a Minister Plenipotentiary with a small one. He took his leave, and the Committee agreed to strike out the specific sum to be given to any foreign appointment, leaving it to the President to account, and appropriated 30,000 doll. generally for the purpose.

[1] Boyd, XVI, 381.

AN INTERVIEW WITH MR. JEFFERSON—MARGARET BAYARD SMITH— 1800[2]

"And is this," said I, after my first interview with Mr. Jefferson, "the violent democrat, the vulgar demagogue, the bold atheist and profligate man I have so often heard denounced by the federalists? Can this man so meek and mild, yet dignified in his manners, with a voice so soft and low, with a countenance so benignant and intelligent, can he be that daring leader of a faction, that disturber of the peace, that enemy of all rank and order?" Mr. Smith, indeed, (himself a democrat) had given me a very different description of this celebrated individual; but his favourable opinion I attributed in a great measure to his political feelings, which led him zealously to support and exalt the party to which he belonged, especially its popular and almost idolized leader. Thus the virulence of party-spirit was somewhat neutralized, nay, I even entertained towards him the most kindly dispositions, knowing him to be not only politically but personally friendly to my husband; yet I did believe that he was an ambitious and violent demagogue, coarse and vulgar in his manners, awkward and rude in his appearance, for such had the public journals and private conversations of the federal party represented him to be.

In December, 1800, a few days after Congress had for the first time met in our new Metropolis, I was one morning sitting alone in the parlour, when the servant opened the door and showed in a gentleman who wished to see my husband. The usual frankness and care with which I met strangers, were somewhat checked by the dignified and reserved air of the present visitor; but the chilled feeling was only momentary, for after taking the chair I offered him in a free and easy manner, and carelessly throwing his arm on the table near which he sat, he turned towards me a countenance beaming with an expression of benevolence and with a manner and voice almost femininely soft and gentle, entered into conversation on the commonplace topics of the day, from which, before I was conscious of it, he had drawn me into observations of a more personal and interesting nature. I know not how it was, but there was something in his manner, his countenance and voice that at once unlocked my heart, and in answer to his casual enquiries concerning our situation in our *new home,* as he called it, I found myself frankly telling him what I liked or disliked in our

[2] From Margaret Bayard Smith, *The First Forty Years of Washington Society* (New York, 1906), pp. 5–7.

present circumstances and abode. I knew not who he was, but the interest with which he listened to my artless details, induced the idea he was some intimate acquaintance or friend of Mr. Smith's and put me perfectly at my ease; in truth so kind and conciliating were his looks and manners that I forgot he was not a friend of my own, until on the opening of the door, Mr. Smith entered and introduced the stranger to me as *Mr. Jefferson.*

I felt my cheeks burn and my heart throb, and not a word more could I speak while he remained. Nay, such was my embarrassment I could scarcely listen to the conversation carried on between him and my husband. For several years he had been to me an object of peculiar interest. In fact my destiny, for on his success in the pending presidential election, or rather the success of the democratic party, (their interests were identical) my condition in life, my union with the man I loved, depended. In addition to this personal interest, I had long participated in my husband's political sentiments and anxieties, and looked upon Mr. Jefferson as the corner stone on which the edifice of republican liberty was to rest, looked upon him as the champion of human rights, the reformer of abuses, the head of the republican party, which must rise or fall with him, and on the triumph of the republican party, which must rise or fall with him, and on the triumph of the republican party I devoutly believed the security and welfare of my country depended. Notwithstanding those exalted views of Mr. Jefferson as a political character; and ardently eager as I was for his success, I retained my previously conceived ideas of the coarseness and vulgarity of his appearance and manners and was therefore equally awed and surprised, on discovering the stranger whose deportment was so dignified and gentlemanly, whose language was so refined, whose voice was so gentle, whose countenance was so benignant, to be no other than Thomas Jefferson. How instantaneously were all these preconceived prejudices dissipated, and in proportion to their strength, was the reaction that took place in my opinions and sentiments. I felt that I had been the victim of prejudice, that I had been unjust. The revolution of feeling was complete and from that moment my heart warmed to him with the most affectionate interest and I implicitly believed all that his friends and my husband believed and which the after experience of many years confirmed. Yes, not only was he great, but a truly good man!

The occasion of his present visit, was to make arrangements with Mr. Smith for the publication of his *Manual for Congress,* now called *Jefferson's manual.* The original was in his own neat, plain, but elegant handwriting. The manuscript was as legible as printing and its unadorned simplicity was emblematical of his character. It is still preserved by Mr. Smith and valued as a precious relique.

After the affair of business was settled, the conversation became general and Mr. Jefferson several times addressed himself to me; but although his manner was unchanged, my feelings were, and I could not recover sufficient ease to join in the conversation. He shook hands cordially with us both when he departed, and in a manner which said as plain as words could do, "I am your friend."

10

The Adams Family Views Jefferson

The lively Adams family enjoyed a complicated, changing relationship with Jefferson. The early friendship is recalled in a brief note by the spirited Abigail Adams, while her husband, John Adams, was Jefferson's close friend on their diplomatic missions in Europe. Political differences soon estranged Jefferson and the Adams family—differences that crystallized with the development of the French Revolution abroad and the political divisions within the first administration of Washington at home. The second selection, written on the occasion of Jefferson's resignation as Secretary of State from Washington's Cabinet, shows the bitter hostility Adams then felt toward him. The third selection reports on John Quincy Adams dining with Jefferson at the White House, when the President presided over a brilliant company. The fourth selection, John Adams to Benjamin Rush on Christmas Day, 1811, reveals the serio-comic basis for the rapprochement that Benjamin Rush had been attempting to bring about between the two old friends. The last two selections are from the diary of John Quincy Adams in January, 1831, on the occasion of his reading the newly published volumes of The Writings of Thomas Jefferson *edited by his grandson, Thomas Jefferson Randolph.*

ABIGAIL ADAMS TO THOMAS JEFFERSON—JUNE 6, 1785[1]

Dear Sir

Mr. Adams has already written you that we arrived in London upon the 27 of May. We journey'd slowly and sometimes silently. I think I have somewhere met with the observation that nobody ever

---

[1] From *Adams-Jefferson Letters*, Lester J. Cappon, ed. (Chapel Hill: University of North Carolina Press, 1959), p. 28. Reprinted by permission of the publisher and the Institute of Early American History and Culture.

leaves paris but with a degree of tristeness. I own I was loth to leave my garden because I did not expect to find its place supplied. I was still more loth on account of the increasing pleasure, and intimacy which a longer acquaintance with a respected Friend promised, to leave behind me the only person with whom my Companion could associate with perfect freedom, and unreserve: and whose place he had no reason to expect supplied in the Land to which he is destinied.

JOHN ADAMS TO JOHN QUINCY ADAMS—JANUARY 3, 1794 [2]

My Dear Son,

The Public Papers will inform you that Mr. Jefferson has resigned and that Mr. Randolph is appointed Secretary of State. . . .

The Motives to Mr. Jefferson Resignation are not assigned [?], and are left open to the conjectures of a Speculating World. I also am a Speculator in the Principles and Motives of Mens Actions and may guess as well as others. . . . 1. Mr. Jefferson has an habit as well as a disposition of expensive Living, and as his Salery was not adequate to his Luxury, he could not Subdue his Pride and Vanity as I have done, and proportion his Style of Life to his Revenue. 2. Mr. Jefferson is in debt as I have heard to an amount of Seven thousand Pounds before the War, so that I suppose he cannot afford to spend his private means in the Public Service. 3. Mr. Jefferson has been obliged to lower his voice on Politics. Pain[e]s Principles when adopted by Genet, were not found so convenient for a Secretary of State. 4. He could not rule the Roost in the Ministry. He was often in a Ministry. 5. Ambition is the subtlest Beast of the Intellectual and Moral Field. It is wonderfully adroit in concealing itself from its owner. . . . Jefferson thinks he shall by this step get a Reputation of an humble, modest, meek Man, wholly without ambition or vanity. He may even have deceived himself into this Belief. But if a Prospect opens, the World will see and he will feel, that he is as ambitious as Oliver Cromwell though no soldier. 6. At other moments he may meditate the gratification of his ambition. . . . And if Jefferson after the Death or Resignation of the President should be summoned from the familiar Society of Egeria to govern the country forty years in Peace and Piety, So be it. 7. The Tide of popular Sentiment in Virginia runs not so rapidly in favor of Jacobinical feelings as it did—though the Party were a Majority and carried every Member at the last Elections, there are Symptoms of increasing federalism in Virginia. A wise man like Jefferson fore-

[2] The Adams Papers, Microfilm Reel 376.

seeth the EVIL and hideth himself.—But after all I am not very anxious what were his motives—tho his Desertion may be a loss to us of Lame Talents, I am not sorry for it on the whole, because his soul is poisoned with ambition and Temper imbittered against the . . . Administration. . . .

See this is confidential

I am, Affectionately yours,

DIARY OF JOHN QUINCY ADAMS—NOVEMBER 23, 1804 [3]

— . . . Dined with the President. Mrs. Adams did not go. The company were Mr. R. Smith, Secretary of the Navy, and his lady, Mr. and Mrs. Harrison, Miss Jenifer and Miss Mouchette, Mr. Brent, and the President's two sons-in-law, with Mr. Burwell, his private secretary. I had a good deal of conversation with the President. The French Minister just arrived had been this day first presented to him, and appears to have displeased him by the profusion of gold lace on his clothes. He says they must get him down to a plain frock coat, or the boys in the streets will run after him as a sight. I asked if he had brought his *Imperial* credentials, and was answered he had. Mr. Jefferson then turned the conversation towards the French Revolution, and remarked how *contrary to all expectation* this great *bouleversement* had turned out. It seemed as if every thing in that country for the last twelve or fifteen years had been a DREAM; and who could have imagined that such an *ébranlement* would have come to this? He thought it very much to be wished that they could now return to the Constitution of 1789, and call back *the Old Family*. For although by that Constitution the Government was much too weak, and although it was defective in having a Legislature in only one branch, yet even thus it was better than the present form, where it was impossible to perceive *any limits*. I have used as near as possible his very words; for this is one of the most unexpected phases in the waxing and waning opinions of this gentleman concerning the French Revolution. He also mentioned to me the extreme difficulty he had in finding fit characters for appointments in Louisiana, and said he would now give *the creation* for a young lawyer of good abilities, and who could speak the French language, to go to New Orleans as one of the Judges of the Superior Court in the Territory. The salary was about two thousand dollars. We had been very lucky in obtaining one such Judge in

[3] From *The Diary of John Quincy Adams, 1794–1845*, Allan Nevins, ed. (New York: Longmans, Green and Co., 1928), pp. 24–26.

Mr. Prevost of New York, who had accepted the appointment, and was perfectly well qualified, and he was in extreme want of another. I could easily have named a character fully corresponding to the one he appeared so much to want. But if his observations were meant as a *consultation* or an intent to ask whether I knew any such person I could recommend, he was not sufficiently explicit. Though if they were not, I know not why he made them to me. He further observed that both French and Spanish ought to be made primary objects of acquisition in all the educations of our young men. As to Spanish, it was so easy that he had learned it, with the help of a Don Quixote lent him by Mr. Cabot, and a grammar, in the course of a passage to Europe, on which he was but nineteen days at sea. But Mr. Jefferson tells large stories. At table he told us that when he was at Marseilles he saw there a Mr. Bergasse, a famous manufacturer of wines, who told him that he would make him any sort of wine he would name, and in any quantities, at six or eight sols the bottle. And though there should not be a drop of the genuine wine required in his composition, yet it should so perfectly imitate the taste that the most refined connoisseur should not be able to tell which was which. You never can be an hour in this man's company without something of the marvellous like these stories. His genius is of the old French school. It conceives better than it combines. He showed us, among other things, a Natural History of Parrots, in French, with colored plates very beautifully executed.

JOHN ADAMS TO BENJAMIN RUSH—DECEMBER 25, 1811[4]

. . . I perceive plainly enough, Rush, that you have been teasing Jefferson to write to me, as you did me some time ago to write to him. You gravely advise me "to receive the olive branch," as if there had been war; but there has never been any hostility on my part, nor that I know, on his. When there has been no war, there can be no room for negotiations of peace.

Mr. Jefferson speaks of my political opinions; but I know of no difference between him and myself relative to the Constitution, or to forms of government in general. In measures of administration, we have differed in opinion. I have never approved the repeal of the judicial law, the repeal of the taxes, the neglect of the navy; and I have always believed that his system of gunboats for a national defence was defective. To make it complete, he ought to have taken a hint from Molière's *"Femmes précieuses,"* or his learned ladies, and ap-

[4] Memorial Edition, VII, 81–82.

pointed three or four brigades of horse, with a Major General, and three or four brigadiers, to serve on board his galleys of Malta. I have never approved his non-embargo, or any non-intercourse, or non-importation laws.

But I have raised no clamors nor made any opposition to any of these measures. The nation approved them; and what is my judgment against that of the nation? On the contrary, he disapproved of the alien law and sedition law, which I believed to have been constitutional and salutary, if not necessary.

He disapproved of the eight per cent loan, and with good reason. For I hated it as much as any man, and the army, too, which occasioned it. He disapproved, perhaps, of the partial war with France, which I believed, as far as it proceeded, to be a holy war. He disapproved of taxes, and perhaps the whole scheme of my administration, &c., and so perhaps did the nation. But his administration and mine are passed away into the dark backwards, and are now of no more importance than the administration of the old Congress in 1774 and 1775.

We differed in opinion about the French Revolution. He thought it wise and good, and that it would end in the establishment of a free republic. I saw through it, to the end of it, before it broke out, and was sure it could end only in a restoration of the Bourbons, or a military despotism, after deluging France and Europe in blood. In this opinion I differed from you as much as from Jefferson; but all this made me no more of an enemy to you than to him, nor to him than to you. I believe you both to mean well to mankind and your country. I might suspect you both to sacrifice a little to the infernal Gods, and perhaps unconsciously to suffer your judgments to be a little swayed by a love of popularity, and possibly by a little spice of ambition.

In point of republicanism, all the difference I ever knew or could discover between you and me, or between Jefferson and me, consisted,

1. In the difference between speeches and messages. I was a monarchist because I thought a speech more manly, more respectful to Congress and the nation. Jefferson and Rush preferred messages.

2. I held levees once a week, that all my time might not be wasted by idle visits. Jefferson's whole eight years was a levee.

3. I dined a large company once or twice a week. Jefferson dined a dozen every day.

4. Jefferson and Rush were for liberty and straight hair. I thought curled hair was as republican as straight.

In these, and a few other points of equal importance, all miserable frivolities, that Jefferson and Rush ought to blush that they ever laid any stress upon them, I might differ; but I never knew any points of more consequence on which there was any variation between us.

You exhort me to "forgiveness and love of enemies," as if I considered, or had ever considered, Jefferson as my enemy. This is not so; I have always loved him as a friend. If I ever received or suspected any injury from him, I have forgiven it long and long ago, and have no more resentment against him than against you. . . .

But why do you make so much ado about nothing? Of what use can it be for Jefferson and me to exchange letters? I have nothing to say to him, but to wish him an easy journey to heaven, when he goes, which I wish may be delayed as long as life shall be agreeable to him. And he can have nothing to say to me, but to bid me make haste and be ready. Time and chance, however, or possibly design, may produce ere long a letter between us.

DIARY OF JOHN QUINCY ADAMS—JANUARY 12, 1831[5]

. . . I finished the memoir of Jefferson's life, which terminates on the 21st of March, 1790, when he arrived at New York to take upon him the office of Secretary of State. There it ends; and there, as a work of much interest to the present and future ages, it should have begun. It is much to be regretted that he did not tell his own story from that time until his retirement from the office of President of the United States in 1809. It was then that all the good and all the evil parts of his character were brought into action. His ardent passion for liberty and the rights of man; his patriotism; the depth and compass of his understanding; the extent and variety of his knowledge, and the enviable faculty of applying it to his own purposes; the perpetual watchfulness of public opinion, and the pliability of principle and temper with which he accommodated to it his own designs and opinions;—all these were in ceaseless operation during those twenty years; and with them were combined a rare mixture of infidel philosophy and epicurean morals, of burning ambition and of stoical self-control, of deep duplicity and of generous sensibility, between which two qualities, and a treacherous and inventive memory, his conduct towards his rivals and opponents appears one tissue of inconsistency. His treatment of Washington, of Knox, of my father, of Hamilton, of Bayard, who made him President of the United States, and, lastly, of me, is marked with features of perfidy worthy of Tiberius Caesar or Louis the Eleventh of France. This double-dealing character was often

[5] *Op. cit.*, p. 409.

imputed to him during his life, and was sometimes exposed. His letter to Mazzei, and the agonizing efforts which he afterwards made to explain it away; his most insidious attack upon my father with his never-ceasing professions of respect and affection for his person and character; and his letter to Giles concerning me, in which there is scarcely a single word of truth—indicate a memory so pandering to the will that in deceiving others he seems to have begun by deceiving himself.

DIARY OF JOHN QUINCY ADAMS—JANUARY 27, 1831[6]

. . . In the evening I read a few pages of Jefferson's correspondence . . . Mr. Jefferson's love of liberty was sincere and ardent—not confined to himself, like that of most of his fellow slave-holders. He was above that execrable sophistry of the South Carolinian nullifiers, which would make of slavery the corner-stone to the temple of liberty. He saw the gross inconsistency between the principles of the Declaration of Independence and the fact of negro slavery, and he could not, or would not, prostitute the faculties of his mind to the vindication of that slavery which from his soul he abhorred. Mr. Jefferson had not the spirit of martyrdom. He would have introduced a flaming denunciation of slavery into the Declaration of Independence, but the discretion of his colleagues struck it out. He did insert a most eloquent and impassioned argument against it in his Notes upon Virginia; but on that very account the book was published almost against his will. He projected a plan of general emancipation in his revision of the Virginian laws, but finally presented a plan of leaving slavery precisely where it was. And in his memoirs he leaves a posthumous warning to the planters, that they must at no distant day emancipate their slaves, or that worse will follow; but he withheld the publication of his prophecy till he should himself be in the grave.

[6] *Op. cit.,* p. 412.

11

The Federalist Opposition Views Jefferson—Hamilton and Marshall

The measure of a great man, especially in politics, cannot be taken without considering the nature and quality of his opponents. In any objective history of the early Republic two great figures must be present—Alexander Hamilton and John Marshall. The intense and principled opposition between Hamilton and Jefferson during the 1790s led to the formation of the first two political parties of national scope in the United States. His strategic management of the Republican Party led Jefferson to become President under an oath administered by the Chief Justice, John Marshall, in March, 1801. The classic enmity that developed between the President and the Chief Justice embittered Jefferson's administration and was maintained throughout the remainder of their lives.

ALEXANDER HAMILTON TO COL. EDWARD CARRINGTON—MAY, 1792[1]

Mr. Jefferson, it is known, did not in the first instance cordially acquiesce in the new Constitution for the United States; he had many doubts and reserves. He left this country before we had experienced the imbecilities of the former.

In France, he saw government only on the side of its abuses. He drank freely of the French philosophy, in religion, in science, in politics. He came from France in the moment of a fermentation, which he had a share in exciting, and in the passions and feelings of which he shared both from temperament and situation. He came here probably with a too partial idea of his own powers; and with the expectation of a greater share in the direction of our councils than he has in reality

[1] From *The Works of Alexander Hamilton*, Henry Cabot Lodge, ed. (New York: Putnam, 1904), IX, 528–30. Reprinted by permission of Haskell House Publishers, Ltd.

enjoyed. I am not sure that he had not peculiarly marked out for himself the department of the finances.

He came, electrified with attachment to France, and with the project of knitting together the two countries in the closest political bands.

Mr. Madison had always entertained an exalted opinion of the talents, knowledge, and virtues of Mr. Jefferson. The sentiment was probably reciprocal. A close correspondence subsisted between them during the time of Mr. Jefferson's absence from the country. A close intimacy arose upon his return. . . .

Another circumstance has contributed to widening the breach. 'Tis evident, beyond a question, from every movement, that Mr. Jefferson aims with ardent desire at the Presidential chair. This, too, is an important object of the party-politics. It is supposed, from the nature of my former personal and political connections, that I may favor some other candidate more than Mr. Jefferson, when the question shall occur by the retreat of the present gentleman. My influence, therefore, with the community becomes a thing, on ambitious and personal grounds, to be resisted and destroyed. . . .

JOHN MARSHALL TO ALEXANDER HAMILTON—JANUARY 1, 1801[2]

DEAR SIR:

I received this morning your letter of the 26th of December. It is, I believe, certain that Jefferson and Burr will come to the House of Representatives with equal votes. The returns have been all received, and this is the general opinion.

Being no longer in the House of Representatives, and consequently compelled by no duty to decide between them, my own mind had scarcely determined to which of these gentlemen the preference was due. To Mr. Jefferson, whose political character is better known than that of Mr. Burr, I have felt almost insuperable objections. His foreign prejudices seem to me totally to unfit him for the chief magistracy of a nation which cannot indulge those prejudices without sustaining deep and permanent injury. In addition to this solid and immovable objection, Mr. Jefferson appears to me to be a man who will embody himself with the House of Representatives. By weakening the office of President, he will increase his personal power. He will diminish his responsibility, sap the fundamental principles of the government, and become the leader of that party which is about to constitute the majority of the

[2] From *The Works of Alexander Hamilton,* John C. Hamilton, ed. (New York: John F. Trow, 1851), pp. 501–502.

legislature. The morals of the author of the letter to Mazzei cannot be pure.

With these impressions concerning Mr. Jefferson, I was in some degree disposed to view with less apprehension any other characters, and to consider the alternative now offered as a circumstance not to be entirely neglected.

Your representation of Mr. Burr, with whom I am totally unacquainted, shows that from him still greater danger than even from Mr. Jefferson may be apprehended. Such a man as you describe is more to be feared, and may do more immediate, if not greater, mischief. Believing that you know him well, and are impartial, my preference would certainly not be for him; but I can take no part in this business. I cannot bring myself to aid Mr. Jefferson. Perhaps respect for myself should, in my present situation, deter me from using any influence (if, indeed, I possessed any) in support of either gentleman. . . .

ALEXANDER HAMILTON TO JAMES A. BAYARD—JANUARY 16, 1801[3]

. . . I admit that his [Jefferson's] politics are tinctured with fanaticism; that he is too much in earnest in his democracy; that he has been a mischievous enemy to the principal measures of our past administration; that he is crafty and persevering in his objects; that he is not scrupulous about the means of success, nor very mindful of truth and that he is a contemptible hypocrite. But it is not true, as is alleged, that he is an enemy to the power of the Executive, or that he is for confounding all the powers in the House of Representatives. It is a fact which I have frequently mentioned, that, while we were in the administration together, he was generally for a large construction of the Executive authority and not backward to act upon it in cases which coincided with his views. Let it be added that in his theoretic ideas he has considered as improper the participations of the Senate in the Executive authority. I have more than once made the reflection that, viewing himself as the reversioner, he was solicitous to come into the possession of a good estate. Nor is it true that Jefferson is zealot enough to do any thing in pursuance of his principles which will contravene his popularity or his interest. He is as likely as any man I know to temporize—to calculate what will be likely to promote his own reputation and advantage; and the probable result of such a temper is the preservation of systems, though originally opposed, which, being once established, could not be overturned without danger to the person who

[3] Lodge, ed., *Works*, X, 412–15.

did it. To my mind a true estimate of Mr. Jefferson's character war-
rants the expectation of a temporizing rather than a violent system.
That Jefferson has manifested a culpable predilection for France is
certainly true; but I think it a question whether it did not proceed
quite as much from her *popularity* among us as from sentiment, and,
in proportion as that popularity is diminished, his zeal will cool. Add
to this that there is no fair reason to suppose him capable of being
corrupted, which is a security that he will not go beyond certain limits.
It is not at all improbable that under the change of circumstances
Jefferson's Gallicism has considerably abated.

JOHN MARSHALL TO JUSTICE STORY—JULY, 1821[4]

. . . For Mr. Jefferson's opinion as respects this [judicial] department it is not difficult to assign the cause. He is among the most ambitious, & I suspect among the most unforgiving of men. His great
power is over the mass of the people, & this power is chiefly acquired
by professions of democracy. Every check on the wild impulse of the
moment is a check on his own power, & he is unfriendly to the source
from which it flows. He looks of course with ill will at an independent
judiciary.

JOHN MARSHALL TO JUSTICE STORY—SEPTEMBER, 1821[5]

. . . There is some reason to believe that the essays written against
the Supreme Court were, in a degree at least, stimulated by this gentleman, [Jefferson] and that although the coarseness of the language belongs exclusively to the author, its acerbity has been increased by his
communications with the great Lama of the mountains. He may therefore feel himself . . . required to obtain its republication in some
place of distinction.

[4] From Albert J. Beveridge, *The Life of John Marshall,* IV (Boston and New York:
Houghton Mifflin, 1919), 363.
[5] *Ibid,* p. 364.

12

Madison—His Great Collaborator—Views Jefferson

The prime friendship and fruitful collaboration of Thomas Jefferson and James Madison existed for half a century. It would be hard to find in the annals of political history an equivalent for this harmonious union of sentiment, idea, and action.

JAMES MADISON TO THOMAS JEFFERSON—FEBRUARY, 1826[1]

. . . The awkward state of the Law Professorship is truly distressing, but seems to be without immediate remedy. Considering the hopeless condition of Mr. Gilmour, a temporary appointment, if an acceptable successor were at hand, whilst not indelicate towards the worthy moribund incumbent, might be regarded as equivalent to a permanent one. And if the hesitation of our Colleagues at Richmond has no reference to Mr. Terril, but is merely tenderness towards Mr. Gilmour, I see no objection to a communication to Mr. T. that would bring him to Virginia at once, and thus abridge the loss of time. The hardheartedness of the Legislature towards what ought to be the favorite offspring of the State, is as reproachful as deplorable. Let us hope that the reflections of another year, will produce a more parental sensibility. . . .

You do not overrate the interest I feel in the University, as the Temple thro which alone lies the road to that of Liberty. But you entirely do my aptitude to be your successor in watching over its prosperity. It would be the pretension of a mere worshipper "remplacer" the Tutelary Genius of the Sanctuary. The best hope is, in the continuance of your cares, till they can be replaced by the stability and selfgrowth of the Institution. Little reliance can be put even on the fellowship of my services. The past year has given me sufficient intima-

[1] From *The Writings of James Madison*, Gaillard Hunt, ed. (New York: G. P. Putnam's Sons, 1900–1910), IX, 243–46.

tion of the infirmities in wait for me. In calculating the probabilities of survivorship, the inferiority of my constitution forms an equation at least with the seniority of yours. . . .

You cannot look back to the long period of our private friendship & political harmony, with more affecting recollections than I do. If they are a source of pleasure to you, what ought they not to be to me? We cannot be deprived of the happy consciousness of the pure devotion to the public good with which we discharged the trusts committed to us. And I indulge a confidence that sufficient evidence will find its way to another generation, to ensure, after we are gone, whatever of justice may be withheld whilst we are here. The political horizon is already yielding in your case at least, the surest auguries of it. Wishing & hoping that you may yet live to increase the debt which our Country owes you, and to witness the increasing gratitude, which alone can pay it, I offer you the fullest return of affectionate assurances.

JAMES MADISON TO NICHOLAS P. TRIST—1826[2]

I have just received yours of the 4th. A few lines from Dr. Dunglison had prepared me for such a communication; and I never doubted that the last Scene of our illustrious friend would be worthy of the life which it closed. Long as this has been spared to his Country & to those who loved him, a few years more were to have been desired for the sake of both. But we are more than consoled for the loss, by the gain to him; and by the assurance that he lives and will live in the memory and gratitude of the wise & good, as a luminary of Science, as a votary of liberty, as a model of patriotism, and as a benefactor of human kind. In these characters, I have known him, and not less in the virtues & charms of social life, for a period of fifty years, during which there has not been an interruption or diminution of mutual confidence and cordial friendship, for a single moment in a single instance. What I feel therefore now, need not, I should say, cannot, be expressed. If there be any possible way, in which I can *usefully* give evidence of it, do not fail to afford me an opportunity. I indulge a hope that the unforeseen event will not be permitted to impair *any* of the beneficial measures which were in progress or in project. It cannot be unknown that the anxieties of the deceased were for others, not for himself. . . .

[2] Hunt, ed., *Writings*, IX, 247–48.

JAMES MADISON TO SAMUEL HARRISON SMITH—NOVEMBER, 1826[3]

I have received your letter . . . requesting from me any information which would assist you in preparing a memoir of Mr. Jefferson. . . . Few things would give me more pleasure than to contribute to such a task. . . .

The period between his leaving Congress in 1776, and his mission to France, was filled chiefly by his labours on the Revised Code—the preparation of his "Notes on Virginia" (an obiter performance):—his Governorship of that State:—and by his services as a member of Congress, and the Committee of the States at Annapolis.

The Revised code in which he had a masterly share, exacted perhaps the most severe of his public labours. It consisted of 126 Bills, comprizing and recasting the whole statutory code, British & Colonial, then admitted to be in force, or proper to be adopted, and some of the most important articles of the unwritten law, with original laws on particular subjects; the whole adapted to the Independent & Republican form of Government. The work tho' not enacted in the mass, as was contemplated, has been a mine of Legislative wealth, and a model of statutory composition, containing not a single *superfluous* word, and preferring always words & phrases of a meaning fixed as much as possible by oracular treatises, or solemn adjudications. . . .

The University of Virginia, as a temple dedicated to science & Liberty, was after his retirement from the political sphere, the object nearest his heart, and so continued to the close of his life. His devotion to it was intense, and his exertions unceasing. It bears the stamp of his genius, and will be a noble monument of his fame. His general view was to make it a nursery of Republican patriots as well as genuine scholars. . . .

Your request includes "his general habits of study." With the exception of an intercourse in a session of the Virginia Legislature in 1776, rendered slight by the disparity between us, I did not become acquainted with M^r. Jefferson till 1779, when being a member of the Executive Council, and he the Governor, an intimacy took place. From that date we were for the most part separated by different walks in public & private life, till the present Govr. brought us together, first when he was Secretary of State and I a member of the House of Rep^s.;

---

[3] Hunt, ed., *Writings,* IX, 256–61.

and next, after an interval of some years, when we entered, in another relation, the service of the U. S. in 1801. Of his earlier habits of study
therefore I can not particularly speak. It is understood that whilst at
College [Wm. & Mary] he distinguished himself in all the branches of
knowledge taught there; and it is known that he never after ceased to
cultivate them. The French language he had learned when very young,
and became very familiar with it, as he did with the literary treasures
which it contains. He read, and at one time spoke the Italian also; with a
competent knowledge of Spanish; adding to both the Anglo-Saxon, as
a root of the English, and an element in legal philosophy. The Law
itself he studied to the bottom, and in its greatest breadth, of which
proofs were given at the Bar which he attended for a number of years,
and occasionally throughout his career. For all the fine arts, he had a
more than common taste; and in that of architecture; which he studied
in both its useful, and its ornamental characters, he made himself an
adept; as the variety of orders and stiles, executed according to his plan
founded on the Grecian & Roman models and under his superintend-
ance, in the Buildings of the University fully exemplify. Over & above
these acquirements, his miscellaneous reading was truly remarkable,
for which he derived leisure from a methodical and indefatigable
application of the time required for indispensable objects, and particularly from his rule of never letting the sun rise before him. His relish
for Books never forsook him, not even in his infirm years and in his
devoted attention to the rearing of the University, which led him often
to express his regret that he was so much deprived of that luxury, by
the epistolary tasks, which fell upon him, and which consumed his
health as well as his time. He was certainly one of the most learned
men of the age. It may be said of him as has been said of others that
he was a "walking Library," and what can be said of but few such
prodegies, that Genius of Philosophy ever walked hand in hand with
him.

JAMES MADISON TO JAMES K. PAULDING—APRIL, 1831[4]

. . . It may on the whole be truly said of him, that he was greatly
eminent for the comprehensiveness and fertility of his Genius; the vast
extent and rich variety of his acquirements; and particularly distinguished by the philosophic impress left on every subject which he
touched. Nor was he less distinguished for an early and uniform devo-

---

[4] Hunt, ed., *Writings*, IX, 453.

tion to the cause of liberty, and for a systematic preference of a Form of Government squared in the strictest degree, to the equal rights of Man. In the social and domestic spheres he was a model of the virtues and manners which most adorn them.

13

Jefferson in Retrospect

MEMOIR BY SAMUEL HARRISON SMITH—JANUARY, 1826[1]

The indignant sarcasm of the poet, that, "This world was made for Cæsar," is not founded in truth. The political redemption, achieved by our Revolution, has substituted right for might. And if it be true, that the world is yet in its infancy, those scenes of barbarous violence, which have heretofore given to human affairs their predominant hue, can only be justly viewed as the effect of the imperfect degrees of knowledge incident to the early stages of our being. Such is, indeed, the inscrutable connexion between good and evil, that it may be to these very scenes that we are indebted for the formation of that character, which, in obedience to your wishes, I have undertaken, I fear presumptuously, to delineate;—a character combining the mild virtues of the man, the impulsive energies of the patriot, the exalted aims and beneficent deeds of the philosopher and philanthropist. . . . Pure and benign as were the personal virtues of our associate; extensive and profound as were his political acquiremetic; although in council he was sagacious and in action energetic; although in his private life he was a model of virtue, and in his public conduct a patriot of Roman texture; although, his, perhaps, more than any other mind, excepting that of Franklin, indicated the course which effected and confirmed our Independence, it is in his character of a philosopher and philanthropist that he destined to shine the brightest, and with the most enduring glory. . . .

. . . Heroes, with few exceptions, have been the scourges of our race; statesmen have too generally attempted, impotently, I know, to advance the interests of their own country on the ruin of a rival; philosophers alone, animated by the holy spirit of philanthropy, have, by their precepts and example, led the way to universal happiness; have broken down the barriers that divide nations; have taught us that, as we are the creation of one common God, we should, as one family, be united in one common interest. . . .

[1] From *A Memoir of the Life, Character, and Writings of Thomas Jefferson*, address delivered to the Columbian Institute of Washington (City of Washington: S. A. Elliott, Printer, 1827).

. . . How noble the position of him, who, standing exalted above the passions and prejudices that divide communities, points them the way to peace and happiness! Such is the position in which our departed friend now stands, and will forever stand! Such the solidity of a fame, based on the whole civilized world!

That such was the estimate he formed of the superior dignity of philosophy, and those who cultivated it, will be attested by all who enjoyed his familiar conversation. To a friend, with whom he conversed without reserve, when his popularity was at its zenith, and he was about to leave the helm of state, he observed,—"The whole of my life has been at war with my natural taste, feelings and wishes. Domestic life and literary pursuits were my first and latest desire. Circumstances led me along the path I have trodden, and, like a bow long bent, when unstrung, I resume with delight the character and pursuits for which nature designed me."

There is, on this head, a precious document, the offspring of his pen, in which this sentiment is expressed in such language, that it would be injustice to omit it. In January, 1797, he was chosen President of the American Philosophical Society. On the annunciation to him of this appointment, he replied in the following terms:

"The suffrage of a body, which comprehends whatever the American world has of distinction in philosophy and science in general, is the most flattering incident of my life, and that to which I am the most sensible. My satisfaction would be complete, were it not for the consciousness that it is far beyond my titles. I feel no qualification for this distinguished post, but a sincere zeal for all the objects of our institution, and an ardent desire to see knowledge so disseminated through the mass of mankind, that it may, at length, reach even the extremes of society, beggars and kings." . . .

Of this society he was the pride and delight. His constant attendance at its meetings, while he resided in Philadelphia, gave them an interest which had not been felt since their assembling at the private apartments of Franklin, when too feeble to attend at their hall. The conversations, to which he, more than any other member, gave rise and contributed, made it once more the resort of men whom the strifes of politics and theology had divided; science, under such auspices, began to raise her head, as will appear by consulting the Society's *Transactions* at that period, which were enriched by several valuable contributions by him. . . .

. . . In every vicissitude of life, as well in stormy as in tranquil times, he maintained his devotion to philosophy and science; and it may be doubted whether he passed a day without allotting some portion of it to the acquisition or diffusion of knowledge. . . .

But highly respectable as these productions are, it is not so much for what he has himself written or done, as for that which he impelled, or aided others to write or do, that he merits the approving award of philosophy. Time will not allow me to dwell on this view of his character. As an evidence of the impulse given by an exalted mind, it may suffice to state, that the most powerful prince in Europe felt its influence, and presented the singular spectacle of an absolute monarch, in one quarter of the globe, consulting a republican philosopher, in another, on the best means of extending the blessings of liberty to his subjects. . . .

He was so well acquainted with, as to read with ease, both the great classical languages of antiquity. He was, moreover, an eminent economist, a good mathematician and chemist, a profound historian, a master of classical literature, and well read in theology, especially the sacred writings. Such was the exquisite union of science and taste in his character, that even in his latter days his favourite studies were geometry and the ancient classics. For all the fine arts he had more than a common taste; in that of architecture, which he studied both in its useful and ornamental branches, he made himself an adept; and in music he had in early life been a distinguished amateur. Many of the mechanic arts were so familiar to him, that he frequently, in his own workshop, formed models, or fashioned implements with his own hands. Over and above these acquirements, his miscellaneous reading was truly remarkable, for which he derived leisure from a methodical and indefatigable application of the time required for indispensable objects, and particularly, from his habit of early rising. What he acquired, he learned with such precision, that no man, perhaps, with greater success, imparted his ideas to others. His relish for books never forsook him, not even in his infirm years and in his devoted attachment to the rearing of the University, which led him often to express his regret that he was so much deprived of that luxury, by the epistolary tasks which fell upon him, and which consumed his health as well as his time. He was certainly one of the most learned men of the age. It may be said of him, as has been said of others, that he was a "Walking Library," and, what can be said of but few such prodigies, that the genius of philosophy walked hand in hand with him.

With this rare assemblage of powers, practical as well as theoretical, he combined an enthusiastic devotion to the happiness of his fellow-men. Long as he lived the frost of age never reached his heart. For more than half a century he was the associate, the friend, the patron of learned men. However their foibles may have amused him, he viewed and treated them as the truly great men of the earth, ranking them infinitely above the powers and potentates, whose brief day is, comparatively, but as a flitting shadow. To them he unbosomed himself, and his hand was ever ready to aid them. No feasible scheme of benevolence was, probably, ever presented to him, that he did not encourage; and it may, I think, be affirmed, that he contributed to found more temples for education and religion, than any man living. . . .

On closing this imperfect sketch of a character, to which full justice only can be done by the ample page of history, it may be asked, is it enough to render these perishable tributes to the memory of one, whose example is so replete with instruction to generations yet to come? No, gentlemen, no, there is a duty yet to be performed. An admiring country should erect a monument to his fame; not of marble or of brass—these are the indiscriminate rewards of successful virtue or triumphant vice.—They may have their use. . . . But they are not the appropriate memorials of men, who, by the active powers of their minds, have urged on the glorious career of human improvement. Such men should live in their works. Let, then, a grateful country, through its constitutional organs, cause a selection of the writings of this great and good man to be made, and published with a plain history of his life. Let thousands and tens of thousands of these be diffused throughout the land, that the humblest cottage, as well as the loftiest palace, may be cheered by their light, and may emulate the virtues they instil.

EULOGY BY NICHOLAS BIDDLE—APRIL, 1827[2]

. . . The peculiar character of the mind of Jefferson was its entire originality. There was nothing feeble nor ordinary in the structure of that intellect which, rejecting the common-places which pass, only because they go unchallenged, through the world and seeking for truth rather in nature than in received opinions, examined for itself, thought for itself, and yielded its convictions only to reason. . . . The youngest among the leaders of the revolution and at last almost the only survivor of them, he stood between two generations, and his free opinions which had startled the first race as hazardous innovations

[2] From *Eulogium on Thomas Jefferson* before the American Philosophical Society. Published at the request of the Society (Philadelphia, 1827).

became during his life established truths among their posterity. This combination of an original mind impelled equally by the love of science and the love of freedom best reveals the true character of Jefferson and will best explain his whole history.

It is the first glory of his life, to have been one of the founders of a great and free empire, undoubtedly among the most distinguished events in the history of mankind. It was not, like the beginning of the Roman domination, a fellowship of outlaws, commenced in pillage and cemented by fratricide—nor yet the establishment of the obscure dynasties and the village empires of most of the ancient legislators; but it was the deliberate achievement of the proudest spirits of their age, who, in the eye of the world and at their own imminent hazard, built up the loftiest temple of free government ever reared among men. . . .

It is scarcely less glorious that even among his own great associates he was distinguished by being at once a scholar and a statesman. If, as is unquestionable, among all the intellectual pursuits, the master science is that of government, in the hierarchy of human nature the first place must be conceded to those gifted spirits who after devoting their youth to liberal studies are attracted to the public service and attain its highest honours, shedding over their course the light of that pure moral and intellectual cultivation which at once illustrates them and adorns their country. It is thus that philosophy best fulfils her destiny, when coming from her seclusion into the arena of life she shares and leads in defending the cause of truth and freedom. This is not easy: for many who were conspicuous in retirement have failed in action, over burthened by their preparation, as men sink under the weight of their own armour. But to succeed—to combine the knowledge of the schools and of the world—to be learned in books and things and yet able to govern men, to deserve that most illustrious of all names—a philosophical statesman; this is at once the highest benefit which study can bestow on the world and the noblest reward which the world can confer on learning. This was the singular merit of Jefferson. . . .

. . . In the bearings of his personal character, Jefferson can be safely compared with the contemporary rulers of nations, not excepting him—the greatest of them all; nor need our patriotism shrink from the singular contrast between two men, chiefs for nearly an equal period of their respective countries, and models of their different species,—Napoleon, the emperor of a great nation—and Jefferson, the chief magistrate of a free people.

Napoleon owed his elevation to military violence—Jefferson to the voluntary suffrage of his country. The one ruled sternly over reluctant subjects—the other was but the foremost among his equals who respected in his person the image of their own authority. Napoleon sought to enlarge his influence at home by enfeebling all the civil institutions, and abroad by invading the possessions of his neighbours —Jefferson preferred to abridge his power by strict constructions, and his counsels were uniformly dissuasive against foreign wars. Yet the personal influence of Jefferson was far more enviable, for he enjoyed the unlimited confidence of his country—while Napoleon had no authority not conceded by fear; and, the extortions of force are evil substitutes for that most fascinating of all sway—the ascendancy over equals. During the undisputed possession of that power, Napoleon seemed unconscious of its noblest attribute, the capacity to make men freer or happier; and no one great or lofty purpose of benefiting mankind, no generous sympathy for his race, ever disturbed that sepulchral selfishness, or appeased that scorn of humanity, which his successes almost justified—But the life of Jefferson was a perpetual devotion, not to his own purposes, but to the pure and noble cause of public freedom. From the first dawning of his youth his undivided heart was given to the establishment of free principles—free institutions—freedom in all its varieties of untrammelled thought and independent action. His whole life was consecrated to the improvement and happiness of his fellow men; and his intense enthusiasm for knowledge and freedom was sustained to his dying hour. Their career was as strangely different in its close as in its character. The power of Napoleon was won by the sword—maintained by the sword—lost by the sword. . . . But the glory of Jefferson became even purer as the progress of years mellowed into veneration the love of his countrymen. He died in the midst of the free people whom he had lived to serve; and his only ceremonial, worthy equally of him and of them, was the simple sublimity of his funeral triumph. His power he retained as long as he desired it, and then voluntarily restored the trust, with a permanent addition—derived from Napoleon himself—far exceeding the widest limits of the French empire—that victory of peace which outweighs all the conquests of Napoleon, as one line of the declaration of independence is worth all his glory.

But he also is now gone. The genius, the various learning, the private virtues, the public honours, which illustrated and endeared his name, are gathered into the tomb, leaving to him only the fame, and to us only the remembrance, of them. Be that memory cherished without regret or sorrow. Our affection could hope nothing better for him than this long career of glorious and happy usefulness, closed before the infirmities of age had impaired its lustre; and the grief that such a man is dead, may be well assuaged by the proud consolation that such a man has lived.

THE LIFE OF THOMAS JEFFERSON BY GEORGE TUCKER—1837[3]

If we estimate his intellect by its great result rather than by its particular efforts, we must place it in the highest rank. He was able to keep together, to animate, and guide the republican party, from the time that he became secretary of state in 1790, to 1809, when he retired to private life; during the whole of which period he had undisputed precedence in the love, esteem, and deference of that party, and in the hatred of their opponents. In effecting a revolution of parties, he had to contend against no ordinary men; and if he was aided by fortuitous circumstances, especially by the French revolution, it was only a master spirit that could have so profited by them.

Of the peculiar character of his mind it may be said that it was, perhaps, yet more distinguished for justness than quickness; for comprehension than invention; and though not wanting in originality, still more remarkable for boldness. Over that field of political speculation to which his mind was habitually turned, he seems to have been the most far-sighted of his countrymen in his estimate of the practicability of popular government; and the civilized world is every day approximating to opinions which he had deliberately formed fifty years ago. He was thus subjected to the reproach of being visionary from many of his countrymen, because he had the sagacity to see farther than their obtuser vision could reach; and while Mr. Hamilton, Mr. Adams, Mr. Jay, and the politicians of that school drew their fundamental principles of government from examples afforded by the history of Great Britain and other European nations, he saw that these principles must change, because time was washing away the foundations on which they rested. They looked to the accidents of history, and assumed that the future would be like the past: he to the principles of human action, modified as they are by the progressive changes of civil society. But he looked to the changing character of the soil itself. He saw too, more distinctly than any of his contemporaries, the effects of the rapidly increasing population of these states. He anticipated the melancholy destiny of the Indian race, and cherished the only system which could have averted it, consistently

[3] From *The Life of Thomas Jefferson,* by George Tucker (Philadelphia, 1837), 2 Vols. From Vol. II, Chapter XXII, "His character."

with the safety and honour of the whites. His views of the future difficulties arising from domestic slavery, are yet in a state of probation, and are to be verified or contradicted by time. But on all these great questions there are more and more converts to his opinions, among intelligent minds; and maxims which were once adopted by his adherents with the blind deference formerly paid to the *dicta* of Pythagoras, are now embraced by speculative minds as the discoveries of political sagacity, or the logical deductions of political wisdom. . . .

. . . It is on his merits as a lawgiver and political philosopher, that his claims to greatness chiefly rest: it is for these that he is to be praised or condemned by posterity; for, beyond all his contemporaries has he impressed his opinions of government on the minds of the great mass of his countrymen. He thought he saw the sources of misgovernment in the conflict of interests and of passions between the rulers and the people; and that the only effectual way of avoiding this conflict was, by placing the government in the hands of a majority of the nation. All his political schemes and institutions were framed with a view to this object. Such were his opposition to the funding system, to banks, to court ceremonies, to the Cincinnati, to the independence of the judiciary, to the county courts of Virginia. His zeal in behalf of a general system of popular instruction; of his ward system; of the extension of the right of suffrage, all aimed at the same object of placing the power of the state in the hands of the greater number. It was these objects of his untiring zeal which won for him the title he most prized, "THE MAN OF THE PEOPLE." How future ages will regard this character it is perhaps not given to the present generation to anticipate; but from pregnant signs of the times, his friends have reason to believe that posterity is quite as likely to exceed as to fall short of their own veneration for the political character of THOMAS JEFFERSON.

ALBERT GALLATIN TO GEORGE PLITT AND OTHERS—1843 [4]

GENTLEMEN,—I had the honor to receive your letter of the 4th instant inviting me to attend the celebration of the centennial anniversary of the birth of Thomas Jefferson, the author of the Declaration of Independence. The state of my health is such at this moment as to render it impossible for me to avail myself of your kind invitation. I

[4] From *The Writings of Albert Gallatin*, Henry Adams, ed. (Philadelphia, 1879), II, 603–604.

regret extremely that I should be thus deprived of the opportunity to pay a tribute to the revered memory of him to whom I was united not only by a conformity of political principles, but by the ties of gratitude and of a personal friendship which during a period of thirty years was never interrupted, or even obscured by a single cloud.

The testimony of the "only surviving member of his Cabinet" respecting his Administration whilst President might not be deemed altogether impartial. And the just appreciation of all his public acts, and of his eminent services, from the earliest dawn of the Revolution to the time when he withdrew from public life, may safely be left to the judgment of posterity.

But, as one intimately acquainted with him, and who enjoyed his entire confidence, I can bear witness to the purity of his character and to his sincere conviction of the truth of those political tenets which he constantly and openly avowed and promulgated. How far these are congenial with American feelings and institutions may be inferred from the fact that, although thirty-five years have elapsed since he left the Presidential chair, no man has as yet been elevated by the people to the same station who did not avowedly belong to the same school.

I do also aver that for his elevation he was indebted solely to his eminent public services and to the knowledge of his political opinions; that he was altogether the spontaneous choice of the people, not promoted by any intrigue, nor even nominated by any assembly or convention, but, without any preconcerted action, and yet without competition, selected unanimously in every quarter by the Republicans who elected him.

I might add much respecting his private and public character; but I have already perhaps gone farther than the occasion required.

PART THREE

OUR WORLD LOOKS AT JEFFERSON

The selections that follow present views of Jefferson as seen by our contemporaries on the basis of twentieth-century scholarship and judgment. John Dewey, the greatest American philosopher of our time, who, like Jefferson, made science and freedom his primary concerns, writes on Jefferson's philosophical scope. He establishes Jefferson in the experimental humanist tradition of American thought.

The remaining selections are by American historians who have specialized in studies of Jefferson's thought and career. Bernard Mayo of the University of Virginia recounts in lively fashion the shifting and contrasting images of Jefferson in American history. Adrienne Koch analyzes a significant divergence in the intellectual position of Jefferson and Adams in the years that preceded their estrangement. Dumas Malone, Jefferson's distinguished biographer, deals with him as political leader in opposition to the policies of Hamilton. Julian Boyd, the superb editor of The Papers of Thomas Jefferson, *probes the nature of the enmity between John Marshall and Jefferson. In the closing selection, Adrienne Koch sketches Jefferson's last years of friendship with James Madison.*

14

John Dewey on Jefferson's Philosophical Scope

. . . There is no doubt that Jefferson was the most universal as a human being of all of his American and perhaps European contemporaries also. . . . His curiosity was insatiable.[1] The pas-

[1] From John Dewey, *The Living Thoughts of Thomas Jefferson* (New York: Longmans, Green and Co., 1940), pp. 4–18, *passim.* Reprinted by permission of David McKay Co., Inc.

sage of Terence, accounting nothing human foreign, made trite by
frequent usage, applies with peculiar force to him. His interest in
every new and useful invention was at least equal to that of Franklin.
. . . He occupied practically every possible position of American
public life, serving in each not only with distinction but marked
power of adaptability to the new and unexpected.

The more one reads his letters and other records, the more surprised is one that a single person could find time and energy for
such a range of diverse interests. As a farmer, he kept abreast with
every advance in botanical and agricultural theory and practice. His
notes of travel in France and Italy include the most detailed observations of soils, crops, domestic animals, farm implements and methods
of culture. He is moved by what he sees to design a new mouldboard
for a plough, having minimum mechanical resistance. Just before
retiring from the presidency he notes with pleasure the invention in
France of a plough, which was proved by test with a dynamometer to
have increased efficiency. He was busy in correspondence with European societies and individuals in exchange of seeds. Of his introduction of the olive tree into South Carolina and Georgia and of
upland rice into the same states, he says, "The greatest service which
can be rendered any country is to add a useful plant to its culture;
especially, a bread grain; next in value to bread is oil."

As far as I have discovered, his inclusion of a professorship of
Agriculture in the faculty of the University of Virginia marks the first
recognition of the subject for study in higher education. He himself
ranked it as of equal importance with the professorship in Government that was provided. . . .

There is no discovery in natural science to the credit of Jefferson
similar to that of Franklin in electricity. But his faith in scientific
advance as a means of popular enlightenment and of social progress
was backed by continual interest in discoveries made by others. When
helping his grandson with his scholastic mathematical studies, he
writes to a friend that he had resumed that study with great avidity,
since it was ever his favorite one, there being no theories, no uncer-
tainties, but all "demonstration and satisfaction." . . . His most
active interest was in the natural sciences. The foundations of modern
chemistry were laid during his life time. Priestley is one of the cor-
respondents with whom Jefferson has closest intellectual sympathy.
. . . He was . . . skeptical about theories not backed by evidence
gained through observation, and thought the French *philosophes,*
whose acquaintance he made, indulged in altogether too much un-

verifiable speculation. He says in one letter: "I am myself an empiric in natural philosophy, suffering my faith to go no further than my facts. I am pleased, however, to see the efforts of hypothetical speculation, because by the collisions of different hypotheses, truth may be elicited and science advanced in the end." . . .

While Jefferson's views on the arts, as on science, reflected the preferences of Franklin—and of Americans generally—for the useful and the practical, his standard of utility and of practical value was that of the benefit of the people as a whole, not that of individuals or of a class. . . . In a letter written to John Adams . . . he says that America has given the world "physical liberty"; contribution to "moral emancipation is a thing of the future." Just before leaving France, he wrote as follows in acknowledging the receipt of the degree of Doctorate of Laws from Harvard University: "We have spent the prime of our lives in procuring them (the youth of the country) the precious blessing of liberty. Let them spend theirs in showing that it is the great parent of *science* and of virtue." Jefferson, when at liberty to give his personal interests free range, was much less limited than some of the quotations given above might suggest. The quotations, taken in their full context, are not so much evidence of his personal taste as of what he thought was the immediate need of a new nation occupying a new and still physically unconquered country. If his *acting* principle had been expressed, it would have been: "Necessities first; luxuries in their due season."

Just as it was the "people" in whom he trusted as the foundation and ultimate security of self-governing institutions, so it was the enlightenment of the people as a whole which was his aim in promoting the advance of science. In a letter to a French friend, in which he says that his prayers are offered for the wellbeing of France, he adds that her future government depends not on "the state of science, no matter how exalted it may be in a select band of enlightened men, but on the condition of the general mind." . . . Jefferson's emphasis upon the relation of science and learning to practical serviceability had two sources. One of them was the newness of his own country, and his conviction that needs should be satisfied in the degree of their urgency. Political liberty—or, as he calls it in one place, physical liberty—came first. A certain measure of material security was needed to buttress this liberty. As these were achieved, he was confident that the spread of education and general enlightenment would add what was lacking in the refinements of culture, things very precious to him personally. Jefferson was a child of both

the pioneer frontier and of the enlightenment of the 18th century—
that century which he and John Adams regarded as the inaugura-
tion of a new era in human affairs.

The other cause of Jefferson's subordination of science and arts to
social utility was his European experience. Science, no matter how
"exalted," did not prevent wholesale misery and oppression if it was
confined to a few. In spite of his very enjoyable personal relations
with the leading intellectuals of Paris, his deepest sympathies went
to the downtrodden masses whose huts he visited and whose food he
ate. His affection for the "people" whose welfare was the real and
final object of all social institutions and his faith in the "will of
the people" as the basis of all legitimate political arrangements made
him increasingly skeptical of advances in knowledge and the arts that
left the mass of the people in a state of misery and degradation.

The balanced relation in Jefferson's ideas between the wellbeing
of the masses and the higher cultivation of the arts and sciences is
best expressed in his educational project. Elementary popular
schooling educated the many. But it also served a selective purpose.
It enabled the abler students to be picked out and to continue
instruction in the middle grade. Through the agency of the latter the
"natural aristocracy" of intellect and character would be selected who
would go on to university education. . . .

Jefferson's stay in France gave rise to the notion that his political
philosophy was framed under French intellectual influence. . . .

The fact is . . . in Jefferson's opinion the movement, intellectual
and practical, was from the United States to France and Europe, not
from the latter to America. . . . The real significance of the question of French influence upon him is found in . . . what Jefferson
had to say about the sources of the ideas he expressed in the Declaration of Independence. . . . I believe his statement is to be taken
literally that his purpose was simply to be "an expression of the
American mind in words so firm and plain as to command assent."
There was nothing that was novel in the idea that "governments
derive their just powers from the consent of the governed," nor did
it find its origin in Locke's writings—"nearly perfect" as were the
latter in Jefferson's opinion. Even the right of the people "to alter or
abolish" a government when it became destructive of the inherent
moral rights of the governed had behind it a tradition that long
antedated the writings of even Locke.

There was, nevertheless, something distinctive, something original, in the Declaration. It was not, however, in ideas at least as old
as Aristotle and Cicero, the civil law was expounded by Pufendorf

and others, and the political philosophy of the Fathers of the Church. What was new and significant was that these ideas were now set forth as an expression of the "American mind" that the American will was prepared to *act* upon. Jefferson was as profoundly convinced of the novelty of the *action* as a practical "experiment." . . .

Jefferson used the language of the time in his assertion of "natural rights" upon which governments are based and which they must observe if they are to have legitimate authority. What is not now so plain is that the word *moral* can be substituted for the word *natural* whenever Jefferson used the latter in connection with law and rights, not only without changing his meaning but making it clearer to a modern reader. Not only does he say: "I am convinced man has no natural right in opposition to his social duties," and that "man was destined for society," but also that "questions of natural right are triable by their conformity with the moral sense and reason of man." In his letter to his French friend de Nemours, Jefferson develops his moral and political philosophy at some length by making a distinction "between the structure of the government and the moral principles" on which its administration is based. It is here that he says, "We of the United States are constitutionally and conscientiously democrats," and then goes on to give the statement a moral interpretation. Man is created with a want for society and with the powers to satisfy that want in concurrence with others. When he has procured that satisfaction by institution of a society, the latter is a product which man has a right to regulate "jointly with all those who have concurred in its procurement." "There exists a right independent of force" and "Justice is the fundamental law of society."

So much for the moral foundation and aim of government. Its structure concerns the special way in which men jointly exercise their right of control. He knew too much history and had had a share in making too much history not to know that governments have to be accommodated to the manners and habits of the people who compose a given state. When a population is large and spread over considerable space, it is not possible for a society to govern itself directly. It does so indirectly by representatives of its own choosing; by those to whom it delegates its powers. "Governments are *more or less* republican as they have more or less of the element of popular election and control in their composition." Writing in 1816, he said that the United States, measured by this criterion, were less republican than they should be, a lack he attributed to the fact that the lawmakers who came from large cities had learned to be afraid of the populace, and then unjustly extended their fears to the "independent, the happy and therefore orderly citizens of the United States." Any one who starts from the just mentioned moral principle of Jefferson as a premise and adds to it as another premise the principle that the only legitimate "object of the institution of government is to secure the greatest degree of happiness possible to the general mass of those associated under it" can, with little trouble, derive the further tenets of Jefferson's political creed.

The will of the people as the moral basis of government and the happiness of the people as its controlling aim were so firmly established with Jefferson that it was axiomatic that the only alternative to the republican position was fear, in lieu of trust, of the people. Given fear of them, it followed, as by mathematical necessity, not only that they must *not* be given a large share in the conduct of government, but that they must themselves be controlled by force, moral or physical or both, and by appeal to some special interest served by government—an appeal which, according to Jefferson, inevitably means the use of means to corrupt the people. Jefferson's trust in the people was a faith in what he sometimes called their common sense and sometimes their reason. They might be fooled and misled for a time, but give them light and in the long run their oscillations this way and that will describe what in effect is a straight course ahead.

I am not underestimating Jefferson's abilities as a practical politician when I say that this deep-seated faith in the people and their responsiveness to enlightenment properly presented was a most important factor in enabling him to effect, against great odds, "the revolution of 1800." It is the cardinal element bequeathed by Jefferson to the American tradition.

15

Bernard Mayo: The Strange Case of Thomas Jefferson

In February of 1858 when Patriotic pilgrims braved a driving snowstorm for the unveiling in Richmond of Crawford's statues of George Washington, Patrick Henry, and Thomas Jefferson, historian Hugh Blair Grisby was one of the many orators who extolled these heroes as The Sword, The Trumpet, and The Pen of the Revolution. In the beautiful Greek temple Capitol designed by Jefferson he expressed his "grateful and affectionate veneration" of all three Virginians whom Thomas Crawford had honored "with the eternal voice of sculpture." [1] But it was Thomas Jefferson whom he held in highest esteem, since above all other Founding Fathers "his history is indeed the history of American liberty."

In thus exalting him a century ago Grisby was then in a decided minority, strange as this may seem today when Jefferson is so generally acclaimed, so conspicuously a part of our American heritage. Yet in his time and down into ours Jefferson's reputation has been one of sharply conflicting bright and dark images. His popular image is very bright today, but this is the result of a victory only recently won by his admirers in a long-sustained battle with his many detractors.

The lines of that battle were clearly marked in 1858 when Henry S. Randall published his classic three-volume biography of Jefferson. His reputation, as Randall noted, was "more assailed by class and hereditary hate than . . . all others belonging to our early history —scarcely defended by a page where volumes have been written to traduce it." On the other hand his reputation was "resistlessly spreading, until all parties seek to appropriate it—until not an American . . . dare place himself before a popular constituency with revilings of Jefferson on his lips." Yet in 1858 there also appeared Samuel M. Schmucker's biography of him which, strangely enough, darkened rather than brightened his reputation. Widely

[1] From Bernard Mayo, *Myths and Men* (Athens, Ga.: University of Georgia Press, 1959), Lecture Three, pp. 61–75, *passim*. Reprinted by permission of the publisher.

read and destined to go into several printings, it portrayed a Jefferson who had "a pusillanimous and morbid terror of popular censure, and an insatiable thirsting after popular praise." It well illustrated what Randall called "the leering, sneering" manner "which has been so extensively practised by early and late calumniators of Mr. Jefferson."

Since the forces of darkness were then so powerful, it is not strange that Grisby in 1858 rapturously hailed Randall's biography as the "first great defence in the forum of history of our noble chief of Monticello." For refuting the many works defaming him, "every liberal American ought to thank you," wrote Virginia's leading historian to the New York biographer. "No Virginian could have written the life of Jefferson," since even here in Virginia, even among his own Randolph kin, he still has many "bitter and unappeasable enemies." Regardless of hostile reviewers, wrote Grisby consolingly, "be assured that your day of triumph will come; but whether the time be long or short, I am not able to say."

Far less consoling were letters to Randall from England's leading historian, Lord Macaulay. Randall's excellent biography had failed to change Macaulay's preference for the conservative views of Washington. It had failed to soften Macaulay's stinging indictment of a Jefferson whose democratic principles, so His Lordship grimly predicted, would by our day cause a "fatal calamity" and destroy America. "Your republic will be as fearfully plundered and laid waste in the twentieth century as the Roman Empire was in the fifth," he wrote Randall. "Your Huns and Vandals will have been engendered within your own country by your own institutions. Thinking thus, of course I can not reckon Jefferson among the benefactors of makind." While "your institutions have, during the whole of the nineteenth cetury, been constantly becoming more Jeffersonian and less Washingtonian," said Macaulay, "it is surely strange that while this process has been going on, Washington should have been exalted into a god, and Jefferson degraded into a demon."

In reporting The Strange Case of Thomas Jefferson the historian-detective finds it pleasing to note that the republic has survived to become the democratic leader of a free world which includes Macaulay's England. But to explain Jefferson's dark image is less pleasing, since it suggests that to be great is to be misunderstood, and to be great in American politics is to be grossly abused. For his strange case is unparalleled for its vilification, and for the use and misuse of a great man's reputation.

His degrading into a demon is directly connected with the exalting of Washington into a god by Parson Weems, John Marshall, and innumerable other biographers. . . .

For years after Washington's death his godlike image was exploited for anti-Jefferson purposes by the Hamiltonians. As Washington's diabolical rival, Jefferson was condemned in the many biographies of Washington, Hamilton, and other Federalist heroes on down into our time, in the partisan tradition of Marshall's Washington. This work by Jefferson's cousin, the Chief Justice, published when Jefferson was President and denounced by him as a Federalist libel, long served Americans as a political history. . . .

This degrading process was given impetus in Jefferson's lifetime by his success in advancing democratic principles, a success so marked that the Federalists became the most frustrated politicians in our history. Self-styled "the rich, wise, well-born, and able," they believed that they alone should rule. To them the word "democracy" was a nasty word, akin to "mobocracy" and "anarchy." As such the word was employed by Hamilton when he called on conventional religion and entrenched wealth to save America from Jefferson's "poison of democracy." Washington used it and the equally nasty word "Jacobin," akin today to "Communist," in denouncing Jefferson's criticism of such reactionary policies as the Sedition Law, by which the Federalists would throttle all political criticism. Throughout Jefferson's presidency, for example America's foremost magazine editor, Joseph Dennie of the *Port Folio*, with almost incredible scurrility each week pilloried and ridiculed that "Mammoth of Democracy" in the White House. And as early as 1804 he anticipated Lord Macaulay by declaring that "the fever of Democracy," by corrupting politics and morals, had all but pushed the republic into "the grave which Anarchy is digging for our Commonwealth." . . .

He was darkly portrayed as a ferocious "Frenchified Jacobin," with all the overtones of French Revolutionary excesses, lusting to chop off heads in the name of Humanity and the Age of Reason. Yet he was, as well, the pensioned and cringing slave of despotic Emperor Napoleon. He was as famous for his French red breeches and crackpot inventions as for the "glittering generalities" of his Declaration of Independence; "that false, and flatulent, and foolish" Declaration about liberty and equality, said Editor Dennie, the public reading of which each July 4th should be banned since it only inflamed the masses and gave them ideas above their proper station in life. He was a man befogged by metaphysical contradictions, with vain and silly pretensions to universal knowledge. He was most absurd when spouting forth his moonshine philosophy about the inalienable rights of all men. . . .

Yet dark as was this image pictured by his enemies, in his lifetime the bright image predominated. The evidence is overwhelming. It is attested by his election as Vice President in 1796, his defeat of John Adams in the presidential contest of 1800, and by his landslide victory in 1804 when, with moderate Federalists and independent voters flocking to his standard, he carried all seventeen states of the Union except Connecticut and Delaware. He refused to consider a third term. But his Virginia Dynasty of national Republican leadership continued on for sixteen more years under his lieutenants Madison and Monroe. . . .

In spite of his many broadcloth enemies, he was indeed the homespun people's beloved President. Republican editors, orators, and liberal clergymen—ever grateful to him as the champion of religious freedom—more than held their own in combatting his foes and extravagantly praising him to the skies. Typical was John Beckley's widely reprinted pamphlet biography of 1800, in which one by one he refuted Federalist charges and slanders. These he attributed to their jealousy of his unrivalled and many-sided talents; to their fear that as President "every germ of monarchy and aristocracy . . . will dissipate at the electrical touch of his republican virtues"; and to their anger "that notwithstanding all their distractious efforts, he continues to possess the unshaken and undiminished confidence of the great body of the American people." For the people know him well as "a man of pure, ardent, and unaffected piety; . . . of an enlightened mind and superior wisdom; the adorer of our God; the patriot of his country; and the friend and benefactor of the whole human race."

For years this bright image was presented in hamlets from Maine to Georgia, from seaport towns to frontier clearings. In many a song "Columbia's sons" rejoiced that to tyrants they would never bend the knee, but always "join with heart and soul and voice, for Jefferson and Liberty." . . .

When he died . . . on July 4th, 1826, his image flamed brightly. A nation celebrating on that same day its Jubilee of the 50th anniversary of his Declaration of Independence marveled at this miraculous coincidence. It was made even more singular by the death of John Adams on that same Fourth of July. Both Adams and the Author of the Great Declaration for months thereafter were fulsomely eulogized by countless orators. The country has gone "Commemoration Mad!" exclaimed old Timothy Pickering, who detested both Adams and Jefferson; even some Federalists have joined in this "present popular mania" for extolling "the Moonshine philosopher of Monticello." It seemed in 1826 that this "Heaven-sent union" in death of Federalist John Adams and Republican Thomas Jefferson was a God-given sign. America's

Revolutionary Epoch was now closed. Old partisan rivalries were at last ended. A new age had dawned in which only the virtues of a dead Jefferson, now enshrined with the deified Washington, would henceforth be commemorated.

But The Strange Case of Thomas Jefferson was far from being closed. Old John Adams spoke truly when on his deathbed he muttered, "Thomas Jefferson still lives." For three years later, when four volumes of his papers were published, Jefferson spoke out from the grave, and with explosive effect. Very frankly written, in all "the warmth and freshness of fact and feeling" of the moment, as he once said, his letters gave his wide-ranging views on most of the controversial issues of America's first fifty years of quick-changing development. Men of the Federalist tradition cried out in anguish at his criticisms of the sainted Washington, of Hamilton and other opponents. To combat him they published defensive and partisan biographies and writings. And thus Jefferson still lived on, in a renewed battle of contending mythologies.

Even more significant was the use and misuse of his bright image by partisan rivals who would exploit his name and fame. His writings of 1829, and a fuller edition of 1853, became like the Bible an arsenal of arguments from which men of opposing views selected, and excluded, what suited their own purposes. In thus seizing upon his opinions which supported, or seemed to support, what they themselves advocated, they made him a football of partisan politics. They obscured the real man, and damaged his reputation by making him appear to sustain every side of every question, to appear all things to all men.

The Jacksonian Democrats, for example, claimed him as their very own, and used his views to support their laissez-faire, states rights and, on occasion, nationalistic policies. In this they vied with Clay's National Republicans, later known as Whigs, who also claimed him as their party symbol. At the same time he was claimed by Calhoun's anti-national Nullifiers of South Carolina, despite Madison's sharp protest that Calhoun was perverting not only the states rights views Jefferson and himself had expressed in the Virginia and Kentucky Resolutions of 1798 but Jefferson's basic and vital principle of majority rule.

Champions of the Old South used his states rights views as a defensive weapon. But they rejected as "glittering generalities" his basic principles of the Declaration of Independence that "all men are created equal" and have inalienable rights. Abolitionists abused him as a slaveholder. But they made effective use of his inalienable rights and his many denunciations of slavery. The Democratic party long used him as its father-image. But it was challenged by the new major party formed in 1854 which appropriated the very name of his old Republican party. Its chieftain, Abraham Lincoln, a democratic nationalist in the Clay tradition, held high the banner of a Jefferson whose principles, he declared, "are the definitions and axioms of free society . . . applicable to all men and all times." But against Lincoln, Southerners who in the 1860s fought for their independence cited as precedent Jefferson's Declaration of 1776, which had justified secession from Britain.

As a result of this confusion of symbols and myths, this welter of half-truths and distortions, the frankly-spoken, complex, and many-sided Jefferson was made to appear the most inconsistent of men. Of his many symbols which partisans used, and misused, most firmly established was that of states rights, with its various connotations. When states rights with its connotations of nullification and disunion met defeat at Appomattox his popularity declined. It was low in the Age of Big Business and of Robber Barons, which made Hamilton its hero. . . .

Most surprising in this Strange Case of Thomas Jefferson is to find his dark image predominating in the liberal Age of the Progressive Movement. The man had become obscured indeed by conflicting myths, his basic philosophy fragmentized and twisted out of context. His states rights symbol as one connoting laissez-faire negativism, opposed to using national power for the national good, was so rigidly established that he was unappreciated by a Woodrow Wilson and despised by a Theodore Roosevelt. Both of these progressives sought to reach goals which in reality were those of Jefferson. Yet both praised not Jefferson but Hamilton, whose nationalistic methods they used to attain their Jeffersonian ends. Wilson thought Hamilton "easily the ablest" of the Founding Fathers. Roosevelt could say nothing harsher of William Jennings Bryan than that he was as "cheap and shallow" as Thomas Jefferson. And Herbert Croly, brain-truster for the Progressive Epoch, likewise condemned his "intellectual superficiality and insincerity." Even darker was his image in the conservative Age of Calvin Coolidge. All too typical was the address given at Mr. Jefferson's University of Virginia in the 1920s by Secretary of State Frank B. ("Nervous Nellie") Kellogg, in which he said that while Jefferson was a great man and all that, his ideas were dangerously radical.

Yet it was in these same 1920s that the day of triumph predicted in 1858 by Grigsby at last began to dawn for his "noble chief of Monticello." That bright dawn was heralded in 1925 by Claude G. Bowers' partisan and popular *Jefferson and Hamilton*. While it glorified Jefferson, it was a refreshing antidote to the many volumes then exalting Hamilton as the hero of an epoch typified by Coolidge's remark that "the business of America is business." A movement then began which has so brightened Jefferson's popular image, not as a partisan hero but as the supreme symbol of democracy, that today he equals, and for many even eclipses, Washington as a national hero. That movement gathered impetus in the New Deal 1930s, reached a peak in the Jefferson Bicentennial of wartime 1943, and still retains its momentum in the cold war 1950s.

Jefferson has been honored by a magnificent memorial in Washington. His Monticello, for a century neglected and its tombstone mutilated, is now restored as a shrine to which come each year over 250,000 patriotic pilgrims. Volume after volume of his writings superbly edited by Julian P. Boyd are coming off the press to be met with critical acclaim. Monograph after monograph by numerous scholars have revealed almost every phase of his many-faceted career. And of the many recent biographies, that in progress by Dumas Malone, by its detailed and judicious scholarship promises to do for our appreciative generation what Randall's classic work of 1858 did for earlier and unappreciative Americans.

Because of this impressive recent scholarship the man as reality rather than myth is much more clearly seen. . . . His bright image predominates today because he is so conspicuously a part of our continuing and usable American heritage. It predominates because in our critical epoch, as in his own Age of Anxiety and social upheaval, the democracy he symbolizes has been severely tested, thus far successfully, by economic depression, world war, and today's struggle against totalitarian tyranny. By deepening our knowledge of him, and of the men and events of his Revolutionary Epoch, recent and extensive scholarship has revealed him to be the most contemporary of the Founding Fathers, as best symbolizing the ideals of both the Revolution and of present-day democracy. Jefferson still lives, as John Adams truly said, because he dealt with basic issues as pertinent to free society in our day as in his, and in timeless manner still speaks with inspiring eloquence for that democracy we would preserve and advance.

16

Adrienne Koch: Jefferson and Adams in the Revolutionary Period

... John Adams and Thomas Jefferson ... were
... the indispensable philosopher-statesmen of the American Enlightenment.[1] They carried on a lifelong inquiry into politics; and they
were continuously and conspicuously present on the public scene, or
at the head of public affairs for four decades—Adams from the 1760's
to the opening of the new century; Jefferson from the 1770's through
the first decade of the nineteenth century. The impress they left on
the American political tradition was extensive and profound—not
only by way of thought but also through practical programmes to
create a durable new political system. Finally, the fact that there were
areas of firm agreement and yet sharp differences between them helps
us to see the tensions that were alive in the thought of their day. We
are made to feel the shock of real alternatives in the formative years
of the democratic experiment and thus more able to see history in
terms other than that of a flat and fictive "determinism."

Adams and Jefferson, as a result of their early emergence as leaders
in the cause of liberty, were elected to represent their colonies at the
Continental Congress. In its famous second year (1776), they found
themselves on the same committee charged with drafting a declaration
of independence. They were both known at this time as "radicals" in
the patriot movement. Jefferson was chosen to write the Declaration
of Independence, and Adams became its powerful defender and
champion on the floor of Congress, his leadership in debate convinc-
ing Jefferson from thence forward that this little Massachusetts lawyer
was capable of real greatness. A "colossus" he called him, for his
energy and intellectual command in the debate. The matrix of their
personal friendship lay here—in the mutual respect for talents dedi-

[1] From Adrienne Koch, "The Contest of Democracy and Aristocracy in the American Enlightenment," *Transactions of the First International Congress on the
Enlightenment, III* (Geneve, 1963), pp. 1000–13, 1015–18. Reprinted by permission of
the author.

138

cated to serve their country, and for individual style. In so many other ways, they already differed and would continue to differ as occasions became piled high with difficulties.

Since there is a general view that the Declaration is simply a copy of the political philosophy of John Locke, there may be some value in commenting on this point. The truth of the matter is that a wholly new element was introduced into natural rights philosophy in the American document. Its opening words cue us to the novelty of the case: the opinion of mankind is solicited, as a court of judgment on the justice of the American cause and the need to wage a revolutionary struggle to defend it. Recall that there was no precedent in history for such a document. No colony had ever advanced a reasoned statement of its need and decision to rebel from an imperial power.

The ensuing political philosophy is also irreducible to earlier models and discontinuous with earlier feelings and sentiments. Men are declared to be born equal, with natural rights among which are specified the rights to "life, liberty and the pursuit of happiness." No public document had ever employed language pointing to this kind of moral ideal—the individual pursuit of happiness. *Property* had been invoked in the past; public happiness had been stated as the *theoretical* objective of a lawful or good government. But the individual right to pursue happiness and to include in its scope the techniques and deliberations required for constant participation in self-government, suggested a fuller meaning for the individual person. The individual became really individual by social partnership with others, selecting officials, scrutinizing the rules of government, deciding when, why and how to alter or abolish them. Also, unlike property, "the pursuit of happiness" has no class boundary. It is thus neither an exclusive privilege, nor is it a merely formal ideal. . . .

The upshot of the thinking that permeates the philosophical sections as well as the statement of particular and local "grievances" in the Declaration is a tough new political logic: government *by consent*, or government *without and possibly against* consent. In short, freedom or tyranny. This hard new political logic embodied what came to be called "the principles of 1776." . . .

In the service of these aspirations, it is a fact that Adams and Jefferson worked together, supporting each other in brilliant complementarity. The Massachusetts intellectual and his Virginia colleague were foremost in giving these "principles of 1776" philosophical definition, recognizing that the issuing of manifestos represented only the beginning of their work. Freedom—not rebellion—was the desired goal. For this it was necessary to do more than win the revolutionary struggle. The whole object of the present controversy, Jefferson said, was to draft good republican constitutions for the states: "for should a bad government be instituted for us in future, it had been as well to have accepted at first the bad one offered to us from beyond the water without the risk and expense of contest." Adams, if anything, was even more insistent. He himself noted that "almost every day I had something to say about Advizing the States to institute Governments" and he was anguished at the vision of an independence that could become a merely destructive movement—"Sampson, pulling down, unless the people also—preferably first—build up the house in which they will live."

Thus Adams would not content himself with the fact that Congress adopted his resolution recommending that the colonies assume all the powers of government. He hastened to compose a small dissertation, in the form of a letter originally addressed to George Wythe of Virginia. This letter was in fact an essay on republican government and on how to construct a permanent constitutional framework, providing for elective, limited and balanced government. . . . Adams's creative encounter with lawgiving proved to be extensively influential in the constitutions adopted by the various states. He also became the principal architect of the Massachusetts constitution of 1780. . . .

Jefferson too proceeded to the constructive phase of the programme. In the spring of 1776, from Congress where he was a delegate, Jefferson sent a draft of a constitution for Virginia to the Virginia convention. It arrived late in the convention's work; nonetheless it adopted Jefferson's preamble and several other features. But it was in the autumn of 1776 that Jefferson assumed the Herculean task of the revisal of Virginia's laws. His aim was to bring the laws of his state into conformity with republican principles. In this vast work he was associated with the finest legal minds in America—especially George Wythe and Edmund Pendleton, but Jefferson by himself drafted 126 bills—a system, as he described it in his autobiography, "by which every fibre would be eradicated of ancient or future aristocracy; and a foundation laid for a government truly republican."

Most momentous of all the bills in the revisal of 1779 was the one which Julian Boyd has described as "Jefferson's declaration of intellectual and spiritual independence"—the Bill for establishing religious freedom. This bill, when enacted into law in 1786, was sent to Jefferson in Paris by Madison, who had laboured tirelessly to ensure its passage. Jefferson then had it printed separately in France, where it became a treasured symbol of the new political spirit to Enlightened thinkers there and throughout Europe. Démeunier, brother of Louis

XVI, inserted the full text of the Act in his article on the United States for the *Encyclopédie méthodique,* calling it an example of "the most limitless tolerance that has ever been seen in any country on earth." Jefferson did not exaggerate to Madison when he reported extraordinary enthusiasm in France for the "Philosophical legislation of Virginia."

The essence of this famous bill is that it defends full and entire freedom of the human mind in providing for religious freedom. Thus, Jefferson's position went well beyond the philosophy of *toleration,* as it certainly went far beyond the practice of religious toleration anywhere else in the 18th century world. Later, he would use the potent phrase "a wall of separation between church and state" to indicate one far-reaching institutional consequence of his position. One recalls that Jefferson had prophetically written into the margin of some notes he was abstracting from Locke's "Letter on Toleration": "where he stopped short, we may go on." The Bill for religious freedom made good the implied promise.

Several other bills were especially valued by Jefferson and his European friends, particularly "A Bill on the more General Diffusion of Knowledge" and the ones abolishing primogeniture and entail. In Jefferson's own summation of the significance of these bills, the one on education "would qualify citizens to understand their rights, to maintain them, and to exercise with intelligence their parts in self-government." The repeal of the laws of entail he intended to "prevent the accumulation and perpetuation of wealth in select families" while the abolition of primogeniture would substitute the equal partition of inheritance, thus removing "the feudal and unnatural distinctions which made one member of every family rich, and all the rest poor."

Whatever else one may conclude about these two representatives of the American Enlightenment, as political leaders and thinkers they were in one profound sense unlike Marx, who in his conception of revolutionary strategy spoke contemptuously of the demand for plans for the society to come after revolution as a demand for "kitchen recipes." On the contrary, Adams and Jefferson had found complete accord in the belief that to revolt without *constituting,* without planning the orderly transition to that "self-government" in whose name the revolution was being waged, was the road to needless turmoil, bloodshed and political servitude. The experiment in popular sovereignty, unless deliberately held to constitutional laws and parliamentary debates and popular discussions on legislation, might be foreclosed, perverted to a greater tyranny than the one they had known. However high the ideals of the philosopher-statesmen might reach, they were entirely realistic about the capacity of any slogan—including the slogan of freedom, liberty, self-government—to become a disguise for new oppressions. Out of loyalty to the free principles of "76," Adams and Jefferson tended carefully their kitchen recipes.

Thus far we have considered the use made of the Enlightenment heritage by Adams and Jefferson as they advanced the moral, social and political meaning of free men. Now we turn to a second period, when the cross-fertilization of "old" and "new" world Enlightenment philosophy enters a new phase. For it was the fate of three outstanding American statesmen to exert strong influence of various sorts while they served abroad as diplomatic emissaries from the United States.

Most celebrated of all was the great Dr. Franklin. . . . Jefferson clearly appreciated the genius of the man he would soon replace as minister to France, and Franklin in turn knew his colleague's worth. He accordingly took Jefferson under his wing and introduced him to his choice circle of friends. On the other hand, Adams and Franklin rapidly developed a cordial distrust of each other, which soon grew into a flourishing hatred. . . .

When Franklin, aged and ill, . . . return[ed] home—Jefferson and Adams remained on the scene as the most illustrious Americans in Europe, to whom the intelligentsia turned for study of America, of the principles and institutions of free society, and, if the truth be told, to observe and take the measure of these men too. Personally, the two Americans who had been partners in the great drama of forging independence, were on admirable and intimate terms. And by a strange coincidence each diplomat, in addition to the multifarious intelligence and information activities which he assumed beyond official duties, managed to publish a book while in Europe. These unusual publications brought the range of American political views into a new focus on both sides of the Atlantic, and provided the occasion for a deeper understanding of political values and measures. It also takes us to the parting of the ways of these two good friends, making them for the last decade of the glorious eighteenth century exponents of conflicting political philosophies and political enemies. . . .

Jefferson's book, the *Notes on Virginia,* had been completed in manuscript when he sailed for France. He had it printed in Paris in English, for private circulation at first; and then it was translated into French by the *abbé* Morellet, who consulted with Jefferson while he was translating, but whose product, alas, was never considered satisfactory by the author. The *Notes* were also published in London in 1787 and quickly sold out, in a country which was still heatedly hostile to things American. Also, Jefferson's book had been elicited by questions put to him by the marquis de Barbé-Marbois, while the latter served as secretary in the French legation in Philadelphia. Both the genesis of the book and its European reception indicate that the Enlightenment had learned to cross and indeed criss-cross the Atlantic! Also the marquis de Chastellux, Jefferson's friend of several years' standing, requested permission to reprint extracts in the *Journal de physique,* which Jefferson granted with two significant exceptions: its "strictures on slavery and the constitution of Virginia." He withheld these, he said, because he was unwilling to "indispose the people [of Virginia] toward the two great objects I have in view, that is the emancipation of their slaves and the settlement of their constitution on a firmer and more permanent basis." This curious small encyclopaedic-type book of Jefferson's, while appearing to be only a series of informative descriptions of the state of Virginia—everything from its topography, flora, fauna, to Virginia's society, history, institutions and habits—had in fact a consistent and unified philosophic perspective. That philosophy embraced several fundamental themes.

First, Jefferson was concerned to defend the American experiment from prejudicial attacks. Most intolerable was that of the abbé Raynal, who added an attack on American culture to Buffon's hypothesis that the animal species degenerates to smaller size in the new world. He asserted that America was not a culture, having produced no great poets, mathematicians, men of genius in a single art or science. Jefferson's reply was itself a token of the kind of pride that never rests content with *any* culture, small or large, the best or the worst. Jefferson wrote: "When we shall have existed as a people as long as the Greeks did before they produced a Homer, the Romans a Virgil, the French a Racine and Voltaire, the English a Shakespeare and Milton, should this reproach be still true, we will enquire from what unfriendly causes it has proceeded." But nonetheless, in military genius he named Washington "whose memory will be adored while liberty shall have votaries"; and in physical science, Franklin "than whom no one has enriched philosophy with more, or more ingenious solutions of the phenomena of nature." His conclusion, however, brings to the fore the American Enlightenment in its distinctive accent. Jefferson wrote: "As in philosophy and war, so in government, in oratory, in painting, in the plastic arts, we might show that America, though but a child of yesterday, has already given hopeful proofs of genius, as well as of the nobler kinds, which arouse the best feelings of man, which call him into action, which substantiate his freedom, and conduct him to happiness, as of the subordinate, which serve to amuse him only." This was his reply to European intellectuals who had passed off prejudice for science and presumed to patronize men struggling for a new freedom. It was the philosophy of "substantiating" man's freedom. This object was primary, preceding in the order of urgency all other matters. Liberate man from oppressive government, encourage him to find identity by recognizing that human existence is a shadowy and incomplete one unless a man may enter at will the political domain of discussion, reflection and self-government. These are essential to human happiness. Even the burdens of self-government will not cripple man's spirit—only the "insubstantiation," the deprivation of freedom can do that.

The more purely scientific concerns in the *Notes* reveal that Jefferson had consciously developed the perspective of experimental empiricism; taking his inspiration from his three moral heroes, Bacon, Newton and Locke. But what is remarkable is that every moral and political question that Jefferson treats carries internal evidence of the respect he had for independent investigation and for applied intelligence. A moderating wisdom of the sort he valued and himself commanded led him, even in the reforms which he most deeply desired, to count the calculable consequences and costs, in human weal and woe. That was why he had stopped to consider whether his strictures on slavery and on the need to reform the Virginia constitution *would do more harm than good.* His distinctive style as a reformer was not that of absolutism: he scrutinized each issue closely, weighing alternatives and sensing the psychological factors of timing, of readiness for reform. Fanaticism, even in the service of supposedly good ends, he recognized as the antithesis of the kind of society he was trying to help bring to birth.

Finally, the core of his political principles, as defined in the *Notes,* makes it clear that Jefferson belonged to that select group of American patriots who took to heart the fully progressive sense of this revolutionary faith. Dr. Benjamin Rush, his good friend, states this position in the following way in 1786: "most of the distresses of our country . . . have arisen from a belief that the American Revolution is *over.* This is so far from being the case that we have only finished the first act of the great drama. We have changed our forms of government, but it remains yet to effect a revolution in our principles, opinions, and manners so as to accommodate them to the forms of government we have adopted." This heightened sense of a *continuing* revolution, the remaking of society by one generation after another, was and is at the heart of the Jeffersonian programme.

John Adams too had taken time to think about America in Europe.

In America, and on both shores he had found that the human heart had its perfidies. So John Adams wrote a book, *A Defense of the constitutions of government of the United States of America,* one which nobody had asked him to write, and for which he made time while American minister in London, nearly ruining his eyesight, his health, and his pocketbook. It was a unique book—a massive, three volume affair, rambling but often eloquent. Its great blemish was profuse embroidery of quotations, pages on end. Overtly this lengthy treatise on political science, with its ill-digested lumps of political history and quarrelsome rejoinders to virtually every great political theorist in the western world, had one dominant motif. Only a properly mixed and balanced government, Adams insisted, could ever restrain men to order and create a peaceful and durable society. Aristocracy (the élite few) and democracy (the many) are, in Adam's language, two ladies "forever pulling each other's caps." Monarchy (the non-partisan "one") is necessary to make the balance in this perpetual imbalance. The ultimate art of government consists in the art of the triune balance.

Clearly, equality is not then a primary ideal for government. How could it be? Men always were and ever will be unequal, in every conceivable way—in brawn and brain, beauty or ugliness, fortune, birth, merit and wealth. Men are equal, Adams concedes in their political rights; but not equally equal! Not uniformly. All, indeed, should have a voice in government, and everyone infallibly *must* be treated equally under the law. But orders among men, differences conferred by the families they descend from are real and ineradicable. To pretend otherwise is to try to deceive men and, in Talleyrand's *mot,* "it is worse than a crime, it is a mistake." It invites men to disregard the rights of property, which are sacred laws if ever there were any. It promotes lawlessness and mob violence, rebellions that once started do not stop until the blood of the people has flowed, and a dictator reaps the profit of the carnage. No, men must learn the truth and learn to *obey* those who are wiser and more learned. . . .

An interesting question is: to whom was Adams addressing these barbed and sometimes impassioned remarks? The answer is, to believing liberals and democrats of every stripe the world over. He especially had in view the dismaying lawlessness in his own state of Massachusetts, as he had recently received from home the news of Shay's rebellion. . . .

But while these events perturbed him greatly, Adams's theoretical effort was too elaborate to be directed at them. Rather, it was a rejoinder to the whole group he identified in his mind as Franklin's

French group—especially Turgot, Condorcet, the *abbé* Morellet—"visionary reformers" who had either no public office or who, when in it, had been unable to maintain their place and power.

One is haunted too by the flitting shadow in these pages of his one-time favourite friend, Thomas Jefferson, whom he may now have begun to associate with the Franklin circle in Paris. Was it this—or was he arguing with Jefferson as surrogate for himself, knowing that they had once had an exhilarating vision of a daring, new-scale political experiment, while it was now Adams's unpopular duty to tell the blunt truth, to warn that the democratic revolution had to be contained for the good of an independent and prospering America? . . .

If these are elements of his doctrine, what had happened to the brave and bold rebel of 1776? Light is thrown on this question by Adams himself, who in his retirement confessed that he was disgusted with the word "rebel." "I was," he wrote, of his part in fighting for independence, "determined never to rebel, as much as I was to resist rebellion against the fundamental privileges of the Constitution, whenever British generals or governors should begin it." Further light is thrown by his frank admission that he had lived through a revolution and in one man's lifetime "one revolution is enough." . . .

If we now move our perspective to the larger scene of the eighteenth century world in the late 1780's, it must be said that Adams sensed very early what a vast movement of social and political revolution was gaining headway on the continent of Europe. He thus provided, through his elaborate work, a rehearsal of the arguments that would later erupt into the great controversy between Burke and Paine over the French revolution and the rights of man. It was precisely in this sense that the *Defence* functioned, both in England and in France.

In Paris, a democratic-republican *refutation* of his doctrine was read by French philosophes before the work itself was translated. An American pamphlet: *Observations of government, including some animadversion on mr. Adams' Defence . . . and mr. DeLolme's constitution of England* by a "Farmer of New Jersey" (John Stevens, in reality) was translated into French in 1789 as *Examen du gouvernement d' Angleterre, comparé aux constitutions des Etats-Unis* (such a revealing title!). The French version was accompanied by lengthy notes and commentary by Dupont de Nemours, Condorcet, Philip Mazzei and several others. We may safely infer then that Lafayette, Condorcet, Dupont and many of their associates were fully apprised of the conservative case against democratic republicanism, before they made their decision to join in the opening scenes of the French revolution and advocate a liberal programme of human rights. They continued to lead the "patriot party" in proposals for the reform of the desperate evils of French society and for the creation of a limited constitutional monarchy, bound by a bill of rights. In these moves, Lafayette brought his group into close consultation with Jefferson, including one rather indiscreet dinner and discussion meeting at the American minister's residence. Jefferson also advised Lafayette and made some changes in his draft of the French declaration of rights. Ultimately, when the French revolution moved far beyond these moderate reformers, Adams concluded that *he* had predicted sooner even than Burke that it would devour its own children.

It is also significant that when the Burke-Paine "round two" of this momentous political controversy broke out in America in 1790–1791, Adams again entered the fray with his essays entitled *Discourses on Davila*—a collection he often referred to as volume four of the *Defence*. This work outdid the earlier volumes as an antirepublic philippic, and used Davila's history to expose the French revolution as doomed to bloody massacre and devastating failure. "Too many Frenchmen, after the example of too many Americans, pant for equality of persons and property" he wrote as about that time. "The impractibility of this, God Almighty has decreed, and the advocates for liberty, who attempt it, will surely suffer for it."

On this volume the fifteen-year friendship between Jefferson and Adams foundered. Each man moved energetically to close ranks with like-minded friends and supporters. The break between Jefferson and Adams quickened the formation of Federalist and Republican parties, the first two major political parties in America. Since the two-party system—or at least two parties—are essential to a genuine democratic government, even their enmity was not fruitless.

17

Dumas Malone: Jefferson as Political Leader

In considering Thomas Jefferson as a political leader, we have to view him more particularly as a party leader. . . .[1]

Throughout most of his mature life he was a public man, but the patriot of the American Revolution who succeeded Benjamin Franklin as minister to the court of France was a high-minded public servant who avoided factional bickerings and whose intellectual interests were virtually coterminous with the world he lived in. In those years he does not look like a master politician, and one may doubt that he really does as George Washington's secretary of state. He could not properly be described as a politician in the common use of the term until after he became Vice President of the United States, in 1797. At that time he was fifty-four years old and had more than a quarter of a century of public service behind him. Not until then did he acknowledge to himself that he was the leader of a party.

In this period he emerged as one of the most effective party leaders in our history. How did this come about? The answer has to be in the form of a story which is in some respects familiar, but which can be freshly told. First, however, we should say something about what he did *not* do and the sort of leader he did *not* become. . . .

To begin with, neither in this nor in any other part of his career was he an orator who swayed men by public speech. . . .

Though he did not often raise his voice, he did ply his pen incessantly, with skill and potency. Yet, even as a writer, he rarely addressed himself directly to the public. . . .

While his reputation was largely based on his public papers, he exercised direct influence, especially in party matters, chiefly through private letters. . . .

He loathed crowds, loved privacy, and built his house upon a mountain. Yet he liked people as individuals and in small groups, and there

[1] From Dumas Malone, *Thomas Jefferson As Political Leader* (Berkeley, Calif.: University of California Press, 1963), pp. 1–23, 25–26, 31–34, 37–41, 52–53, 61, 65–66, 70–71, *passim*. Reprinted by permission of the publisher.

are many contemporary references to his amiability—a thing which cannot be said about Alexander Hamilton or John Adams. He was generous to a fault, exceedingly hospitable, and had rare gifts for personal friendship, but no one would have supposed he had much mass appeal. . . .

The whole field of human knowledge was his province, from the Anglo-Saxon language and Indian dialects to the bones of prehistoric animals. He had one of the greatest libraries of his time. . . . More than any other public man of his time, however, he enjoyed the favor of the intelligentsia, and his enemies tried to turn his scholarly proclivities into political liabilities. In the course of the election campaign of 1796 it was said that he was better qualified to be a professor in a college than to be the President of the United States. Timothy Pickering called him "the moonshine philosopher of Monticello." The most common charge was that he was basically theoretical, and in a sense he was. Few men in American public life have taken general principles more seriously; more often than he should, perhaps, he regarded these as universal truths. On the other hand, he had been schooled from his early manhood in the actual operations of government.

One cannot help wondering how such a man could have become a popular idol, if indeed he did before his presidency. . . .

How, then, did he attain political leadership? The best quick answer is that he never did as many things as his opponents claimed, and that he became a national leader less by his specific actions than by what he was and what he stood for. . . .

His own attitude is characterized by an expression he used throughout this decade and which was conspicuously absent from the vocabulary of the Hamiltonians—"the spirit of 1776." The school of which he was always a devoted alumnus was the American Revolution. . . . The simplest single statement of his own purposes in this confused decade is that he was trying to preserve the fruits of the American Revolution. By force of circumstance his role as leader of the opposition was predominantly defensive, especially in the domestic field. In international matters he was more on the offensive: he wanted to complete American independence. . . .

During the early years of that decade, before he was in a real sense a party leader, Jefferson unquestionably rendered his most notable services to both the republican interest and the popular interest as a symbol. . . . He embodied the spirit of 1776 as fully as any civilian could. He was identified in the public mind not merely with the successful struggle for independent nationality and with anti-British feeling, but with the freedom of individual human beings from political tyranny or oppression of any sort. . . .

The French Revolution was not a divisive factor in American politics for several years after it started. Jefferson reported on its beginnings with notable objectivity while in France. Most Americans appear to have viewed this revolution sympathetically, pleased that the French had taken up the cause of liberty after the American example and given it a new dimension. Jefferson's conspicuous identification in the public mind with the international struggle for liberty was somewhat fortuitous. . . . But the net result was to identify him with the universal rights of man. . . .

The contemporary of Jefferson's who did most to establish him as a symbol in the public mind was Hamilton. Angered by opposition to himself in Congress and by criticisms in newspapers, he charged Jefferson with being the instigator of it all. . . . He built Jefferson up in the public mind as his chief opponent; that is, he established him as a symbol of anti-Hamiltonianism. . . .

When he retired from the office of secretary of state as he neared the age of fifty-one, he said and seems to have believed that he was leaving public life for good. . . .

In these busy years of farming, nail-making, and house-building, he was politically inactive. The major conflict of the period centered on Jay's treaty. His opinion of this he gave in no uncertain terms in private letters: he regarded it as a departure from the policy of fair neutrality, as an ignominious surrender to the British, as a wholly unnecessary sacrifice of American independence for the sake of peace which, in his opinion, was not endangered, and as a major cause of both the foreign and domestic difficulties that ensued. But, in his own state, sentiment against the treaty was so overwhelming that his help was little needed. . . .

He now showed a much higher spirit of partisanship than he had while he was secretary of state. Out of office, he naturally felt freer to speak his mind, but the course of public events had much to do with his state of mind. Following Jefferson's retirement, Hamilton's influence in the government greatly increased, and soon it came about that no Republican voice was heard by George Washington. He and Jefferson had parted on the best of terms and there was no open breach between them while the first President remained in office, but circumstances were driving them in opposite directions.

The fight over Jay's treaty widened the gap which had already begun to open between these two great Virginians, just as it accentuated party feeling in the country. Washington's support of the treaty was incomprehensible to Jefferson, and to him this business, from beginning to end, was a Federalist party maneuver. Controlling the executive department as that party now did, and with a two-to-one majority in the Senate, it had imposed this hateful treaty on the House of Representatives, where the Republicans had a majority, and on the people of the United States, who did not want it. On the other hand, the attacks on the treaty were marked by violence, and in their criticism of Washington the Republicans overreached themselves. . . . In this period of frustration he . . . wrote his famous letter to Philip Mazzei. In this he said that men who had been Samsons in the field and Solomons in the council had had their heads shorn by the harlot England. This was a private letter, addressed to a man living in Pisa and dealing with that man's personal affairs; it did not get out until after another year, when its recipient was so unwise as to give the political part of it to the press. At this stage in our story its importance lies in what it revealed about its author's state of mind. In its bad taste it was out of character, and it is excessively rhetorical, but it describes the political alignment as Jefferson saw it. No individuals were named in it, but it was a sweeping indictment of a group, and from its momentary lurid flash we can glimpse him at his most partisan.

During a period of personal political inactivity, then, his own partisanship intensified, and he became thoroughly convinced of its necessity. A few weeks before he wrote Mazzei, when commenting privately on the conduct and character of his unfortunate successor as secretary of state, Edmund Randolph, he had this to say about parties:

> Were parties here divided merely by a greediness for office, as in England, to take a part with either would be unworthy of a reasonable or moral man, but where the principle of difference is as substantial and as strongly pronounced as between the republicans & the Monocrats of our country, I hold it as honorable to take a firm & decided part, and as immoral to pursue a middle line, as between the parties of Honest men, & Rogues into which every country is divided. . . .

In this mood he approached the year 1796, when the United States had its first contested presidential election. With this, however, he had virtually nothing to do. He did not "run" for the presidency, for under the existing electoral procedure nobody did that. It is hardly correct to say that he "stood" for the office, since he said nothing about it until after the votes were cast. His "nomination" meant no more than that there was a general understanding among the leaders of the party in Congress that he was to be supported. Madison explicitly stated that he did not consult Jefferson beforehand because he wanted to give him no opportunity to refuse. . . .

In the campaign, if we may use that term, he appears to have done nothing whatever, except to furnish some information to friends who were defending him from attack. This campaign is notable on the one hand for the personal abstention of both Adams and Jefferson, and on the other for the scurrilous personal attacks on both of them. . . .

Adams had an electoral majority of three votes over Jefferson, and . . . the latter became vice president. He himself said that this was fitting, since Adams had always been his senior in public life, and that he actually preferred the vice presidency, because it would enable him to spend most of his time at home. . . .

No, it was not a good time to be president, and it would have been even worse for him than it was for John Adams. Diplomatic relations with France were suspended, and the great problem was how to deal with that nation. . . . If the French imbroglio was to be settled, it had better be settled by someone who could not be charged with being pro-French. . . .

The net result of the election was to leave the Vice President as the recognized head of his party and with the prestige of having come within three electoral votes of the presidency. He had no rival in his own party. . . . He found himself in a paradoxical and unprecedented position: nominally a high official of the government, he was also the undisputed and inevitable leader of the opposition to it. . . .

. . . The intensification of partisan bitterness was the rise of the war spirit when the strained relations with France became more widely known. Adams had called the special session of Congress because of the foreign situation, and his appointees as commissioners to France were confirmed at this time. Not until the following spring, when the XYZ papers showed that these commissioners had been insulted, did patriotic excitement pass into hysteria, but already it had sharply risen, and Jefferson's political enemies did not hesitate to revive the old charge that he was subservient to the French. . . .

As presiding officer of the Senate, he was impotent in legislative matters. The Federalist majority in that body, which had been dominated by Hamilton from the beginning of his secretaryship of the treasury, was now two to one, and before the end of the administration became even greater. . . .

In the House, where the Republicans were of approximately the same strength as the Federalists at the outset and where the influence of Hamilton was far less than in the Senate, the unquestioned Republican leader was Albert Gallatin. . . . The policy of the Republicans was to oppose all action which might lead to war; and, with the aid of the moderate Federalists, they kept military preparations down until the XYZ affair threw control into the hands of the Hamiltonians. Jefferson wholly approved of this policy, and no doubt he was consulted about it informally, but there is no indication that he sought to impose his personal will on the party leaders in Congress while he was leader of the opposition. Republican policy seems to have been a matter of consensus, and a high degree of party solidarity was attained in Congress. The Federalists spoke of a "solid Phalanx."

Besides being a symbol, Jefferson served his party at this stage as a rallying center, and by personal relationships contributed to Republican solidarity. . . .

He served his fellow Republicans as a harmonizer and mobilizer rather than as an organizer. One of the first acts that signalized his assumption of leadership was his establishment of good relations with Aaron Burr, who thought that he had been rather shabbily treated in the last election, when as the second man on the ticket he had received a far smaller vote than Jefferson. Burr was no longer in the Senate but was a rising power in the politics of the crucial state of New York. . . . Jefferson as a realistic politician wanted his party to thrive in New York. His advances, by letter, caused Burr to come to Philadelphia to see him. Burr's arrival fortunately coincided with that of James Monroe from France. Since Monroe was in political trouble —the Federalists regarded him as disgraced—a council of war was in order. Jefferson, Gallatin, Burr, and Monroe conferred, and thus the inner circle of Republican leaders was reformed except for Madison— who, however, was kept in touch with the course of events by his friend the Vice President. . . .

After the XYZ disclosures the position of the Republicans was precarious. Circumstances had played into the hands of the High Federalists, who really constituted the war party. Adams himself seemed to be caught up in the war fever, and John Marshall, the first of the commissioners to get home from France, was greeted as a conquering hero. During that mad time Jefferson could do nothing to affect the course of events, and the Republicans in Congress could do no more than hang on. . . .

It need not be supposed that the Republicans and their leaders were always right in their attitude toward specific measures. For example, John Adams was more far-sighted than they in starting a navy. But they were clearly right in their judgment that the dangers of the hour were exaggerated. And they correctly foresaw that there would be strenuous objection to the increase in taxes when the people began to doubt the seriousness of the crisis. In pressing this point Jefferson showed himself to be an astute politician, but he and his party gain their chief merit in history for their opposition to the measures which bore most directly on human liberty and pointed toward what we now call the police state. One was the creation of an unnecessarily large army which, in effect, would have been under Hamilton's command. Since there never was any likelihood that such a force would be needed to repel a French invasion, historians have properly asked what its foreseeable uses could have been. One possibility was that it could have been used in an imperialistic adventure to the southward, against the Spanish and in conjunction with the British. In view of the inflexible opposition of John Adams to this, as well as other unfavorable circumstances, it was only a remote possibility. Jefferson referred to Hamilton at least once as a prospective Bonaparte, but his greater fear was that an expanded army would be used to crush domestic political opposition on the pretext of putting down insurrection. That Hamilton and his devotees would have welcomed the opportunity to employ military force for such a purpose can hardly be questioned in view of what they wrote each other. Credit for blocking the military designs of the High Federalists must be given Adams, and it is a pity that he and his old friend Jefferson did not understand each other better in this matter. But Jefferson sensed the realities from the beginning, and he and his party put themselves on record against a degree of militarism which was intrinsically undesirable and for which there was no demonstrable need.

The Alien and Sedition Acts represented a greater and more immediate challenge to human freedom and the right of political opposition. . . .

In this period he drew several sets of resolutions, highly critical of policies of the government, which became part of the public record, the most important being the Kentucky Resolutions of 1798, but these were presented in the names of others. We may not like this secret procedure, but if he was going to oppose the administration it is hard to see how else he could have done it. . . . The Sedition Act, sought to silence criticism of the President and Congress. (There was no mention of his own office in it.) Ostensibly this was adopted for a patriotic purpose and in the name of public order. As one High Federalist said, "disorganizers" were being arrested for libeling the President and his Secretary of State "to try whether we have strength enough to cause the constituted authorities to be respected." But the real attitude of the group in power was better described by one of their supporting newspapers. This paper candidly said: "It is patriotism to write in favor of our government—it is sedition to write against it." By the government, of course, the editor meant the persons then running it. Obviously the law was designed and unquestionably it was executed with a view to the suppression of a party, the legitimacy of which was denied. This system of suppression was a supreme challenge to Jefferson as a lifelong champion of freedom *and* as a party leader. . . . He believed that something could and should be done on the state level in behalf of liberty and his harassed party. That is, something could and should be *said*. Therefore, he sent to the legislature of Kentucky through a friend a set of resolutions, and he induced Madison to draft a set for Virginia, thus starting a verbal counter attack. . . .

The Kentucky Resolutions of 1798 constitute no well-rounded and well-balanced treatise on federal relations. . . . This was an *ad hoc* document, addressed to a particular situation. Its primary purpose was to start a wave of protest against infringements on human liberty and against the denial of the right of political opposition. The present actuality was that freedom of expression and the very existence of his party, which was to his mind the party of freedom, were gravely threatened. Threatened by whom? By the general government. And if he had not turned to the states for their protection at this time, whither could he have turned? There would have been no point in appealing to the Supreme Court of the United States. That partisan body was no guardian of the rights of individuals, as the Supreme Court is today. At the time the federal judiciary was guarding the group then in power and it left on the pages of history an ineffaceable image of intolerance. . . .

That is, Jefferson invoked state rights in behalf of human rights. He did not invoke them *against* human rights or in behalf of vested local interests; nor did he emphasize them for their own sake. They were merely a means to an end, just as all political institutions were to him, including the Union itself. . . .

It was in the midst of his most crucial political struggle that he said some of the noblest and most characteristic things he ever said. The year after he penned the Kentucky Resolutions he wrote to a student at the College of William and Mary that "while the art of printing is left to us, science can never be retrograde; what is once acquired of real knowledge can never be lost." In this wonderful letter he showed unmistakably that he was waging a more than defensive fight; throughout his career he had been seeking to arrest the course of despotism so that human society might be free to realize upon its immeasurable possibilities. "To preserve the freedom of the human mind then and freedom of the press," he said, "every spirit should be ready to devote itself to martyrdom; for as long as we may think as we will, and speak as we think the condition of man will proceed in improvement." The improvement he envisioned was not infinite, but it was illimitable. In the heat of the campaign, again a prophet spoke.

In the election year of 1800, when the Republican chieftain, who was also the author of the Virginia Bill for Establishing Religious Freedom, was being attacked with unexampled bitterness as an unbeliever, he wrote the words which characterize his purposes better, probably, than any others that he ever spoke. They are now emblazoned on the walls of the memorial to him in Washington, but it was in a private letter to Dr. Benjamin Rush that he made his unforgettable personal declaration: "I have sworn upon the altar of God eternal hostility against every form of tyranny over the mind of man." The now-familiar words may be repeated here as a reminder of the time he used them. But this is no partisan utterance for its own day only. Thus spoke a champion of the freedom on which depend all other freedoms and the progress of mankind. . . .

18

Julian P. Boyd: The Chasm that Separated Thomas Jefferson and John Marshall

"If American law were to be represented by a single figure," declared Oliver Wendell Holmes in a famous address, "sceptic and worshipper alike would agree without dispute that the figure could be one alone, and that one, John Marshall." [1] So qualified, the Olympian generalization could be applied with equal if not superior force to Thomas Jefferson as an embodiment of the democratic ideal. The appraisal testifies to the towering stature of the two men, for law and democracy as two mutually indispensable elements of a free society could scarcely be symbolized by those not possessing qualities of greatness.

But this pre-eminence of Jefferson and Marshall was not grounded in either case upon that distinctive originality of thought by which sharp breaks with the past are reached in the march of human affairs. The Declaration of Independence did for the first time in history declare certain natural rights to be the basis of established political institutions, and the obiter opinion in *Marbury* v. *Madison* did establish a landmark in the development of American constitutional law. Yet in neither case, nor elsewhere, did Marshall or Jefferson create distinctive or original concepts of government. Their greatness in their respective spheres lay in the felicitous combinations of character and dispositions. . . .

Jefferson and Marshall stood in the beginning on common ground, along with the generality of their countrymen. Their divergence in attitude in the immediate post-war years is apparent, though they did not meet until Jefferson became Secretary of State. Even then Marshall's position was so obscured by native caution or other factors that Jefferson, seeking as always to enlist young men of talent on

[1] From Julian P. Boyd, "The Chasm that Separated Thomas Jefferson and John Marshall," in *Essays on the American Constitution*, Gottfried Dietze, ed. (Englewood Cliffs, N.J.: Prentice-Hall, Inc., 1967), pp. 3, 5–6, 8–9, 11–15, 18–20, *passim*. Reprinted by permission of the publisher.

the side of "the republican interest," but dubious of Marshall's convictions, achieved the distinction of being the first to recommend that he be made a judge. The divergence became fixed in the middle of Washington's second administration and was an inexorable gulf by the time Marshall administered the oath of office to the new president. The hostility between the two men achieved epic proportions in the ensuing years, being in no way diminished by the fact that Marshall, during the critical days of early 1801, looked on with less than judicial detachment at desperate Federalist efforts that some believed would place the executive power in his own hands.

Marshall regarded Jefferson as the personal embodiment of "the fatal philosophy of the day," as a man of vaulting ambition who had achieved power over the people by professions of democracy, who possessed a malignant, vindictive nature, and who was an enemy of every effort to thwart the popular impulses that were the source of his own power, being therefore hostile to the idea of an independent judiciary. Jefferson on his part regarded Marshall as the willing instrument of a discredited party that had consolidated itself in the stronghold of the judiciary whence it could loose its partisan bolts at the administration and yet remain beyond the reach of popular retaliation. He thought Marshall a man of strong political ambitions, capable of bending others to his will, determined to mobilize the power of the court by craftiness, by sophisticating the law to his own prepossessions, and by making its opinions those of a conclave which he would dominate. . . .

The cleavage, with its resultant impact upon their respective views of the Constitution and the nature of the union, can best be understood not by measuring its unbridgeable span after the two men came to power but by looking for its source along the common watershed. It was at that point that the true test came. Marshall's own testimony asserts that, on the first signs of boisterousness in the republican sea in the post-war years, he lost "the wild and enthusiastic democracy" with which he had been inspired at the beginning of the Revolution. Debts, inflation, opposition to taxes, commercial rivalries between the states, a temporary stagnation in business, the closing of the West Indies to trade, and, above all, the movement led by Daniel Shays caused him to gravitate toward the position of Washington and other men of substance who looked with anxiety upon the turbulence of popular government. . . . Thus at the first sign of storm, Marshall's enthusiasms for the great experiment waned and he looked for safe anchorage ground under a form of government that promised greater stability of law and order, valuing most that part which forbade the states to impair the obligation of contracts. For him the Articles of Confederation was not a constitution of government but an alliance of states, and it had served only to preserve the idea of union until a substantive law adequate to the exigencies of the nation could be formed.

Jefferson's concern was altogether different. He had anticipated that the voyage would be hazardous: it was a "bold and doubtful election" in 1776 that had committed the nation to the idea of government by consent. When the lowered prospects arrived in the form of Shay's Rebellion and other disturbances, he saw these as evidence that the people were awake and alert. There was no antagonism in his position either to the concept of law or to the rights of property, of course, but he looked for the safeguarding of both to a source that Marshall mistrusted or feared. Our government, Jefferson declared in 1801, was the strongest on earth because it was the only one in which every man would fly to the defense of the law as his own immediate concern. The source of that strength did not seem to him, as it did to Marshall, to be derived from the fabric of government devised in 1787. . . . The strength of the cement of national union on which Jefferson founded his reliance was not to be measured by the extent of powers set forth in a document drawn up in 1787 or by those withheld from a document of 1781: it was to be found in the fidelity of the people to the proposition of 1776.

It was during this post-war period of disillusionment for Marshall that Jefferson proved the nature of his faith. . . . His nationalism was not grounded upon a form of government but upon a faith, and the highest expression of that faith as set forth in the Declaration of Independence was, as John Hancock declared in sending it forth to the various states, the ground and foundation of the government they were to erect for themselves, comprehending thereby whatever form it might become, whether that of an alliance of states which could be made effective by amendment or that of a more perfect union which would wholly dispossess its predecessor. . . .

In no particular is the validity of such an appraisal of Jefferson's aim made more explicit than in the most constructive single achievement of government under the Articles of Confederation—the creation of the national domain. For here, through his insistent effort to induce Virginia to surrender her vast western claim, Jefferson sought to employ the power of a state as he did in 1798 and at other times primarily to achieve a national purpose. No issue in the early period of American history sustains so clearly as this does the divergences between Marshall and Jefferson. Next to the people themselves and the spirit which animated them, land was the great resource on which all else pivoted, affecting with powerful immediacy the attitudes and indeed the livelihood of every citizen. It influenced directly or indirectly almost all of the great matters of policy that came before the government. The fundamental question, once the claims of individual states had been relinquished, was the manner in which this resource would be employed. The national domain contained immense potentialities for the union both disruptive and cohesive, and the choice depended in large measure upon the degree to which one's private interests were submerged in those of the public. On this issue Jefferson determined at the outset of his public career never to join those who engaged in speculative ventures to engross large tracts of land lest his private interests influence or impede his performance of public duty. This was an abnegation for the sake of an elevated concept of the role of legislator that was neither required by the political ethics of the day nor duplicated by any other of the leading figures of the nation. Though its relevance for a jurist was at least as great as for a legislator, Marshall found himself both as an individual and as an expounder of the law most often allied with those interests on which Jefferson had turned his back. The correctness of either course in a legal sense must be admitted. But by his deliberate rejection of the possibility of private gain because of his concern for a paramount public interest, Jefferson provided another measure of an attachment to the nation that transcended mere legality.

The proponents of new republics on the western waters may have been inspired by dreams of great suzerainties for themselves and their families, but in support of their aims they employed the rhetoric and the justifying principles of the Declaration of Independence itself. Were these new sovereignties to be encouraged to set up such forms of government as would "seem most likely to effect their safety and happiness"? Much could be said for this on the score of both principle and expediency, and for a time Jefferson himself entertained the idea without being involved in the economic base out of which it arose. Or, since these areas lay within the territory ceded to the United States by the Treaty of Paris and were thus acquired by the common effort, were they to be regarded as colonial dependencies of the old confederation? This was by no means a new dilemma, for it lay at the center of the debate before the Revolution on the nature of the British empire. Neither extreme was desirable, and so realistic a statesman as Madison thought there was no middle ground between the two. Yet in this age of political experimentation Jefferson and his legislative colleagues proceeded to adopt such a middle doctrine. The new governments would be neither colonial dependencies nor independent sovereignties, but would progress from a temporary status of self-government to organic statehood and finally to full admission to the union on a plane of equality. This great legislative achievement of 1784 which gave to American federalism its distinctive cast, enabling it to expand westward across the continent and indeed into an indefinite future, was a formulation of policy for which no delegated authority could be found in the Articles of Confederation. . . .

While this federative principle for an expanding domain of law and democracy became permanently imbedded in the Constitution, the sale of vast tracts of public lands to organized speculators and the substitution of territorial government administered by Congress for local self-government soon reversed two cardinal points in Jefferson's policy. . . . Retaining for its own committees the right to appoint territorial officers and negotiating with the powerful land group that wished to acquire an extensive tract of public land, Congress for the first time placed in national legislation a prohibition against local statutes that would, "in any manner whatever, interfere with or affect private contracts, or engagements *bona fide,* and without fraud previously formed." Marshall and Washington were by no means alone in making *bona fide* engagements for the purchase of land claims of impecunious soldiers that would thus be protected against legislative whims by the guarantees of a strong-toned government. The substance of this guarantee was repeated a few weeks later in the Constitution, and in abbreviated language that allowed wide latitude for judicial construction. Thus the article that had so strong an appeal for Marshall and provided so powerful an instrument for the protection of corporate interests against state regulatory legislation of the nineteenth century traces its lineage from a policy for the national domain that was the exact reverse of Jefferson's. . . . Its full flowering came in the decision in *Fletcher* v. *Peck* in 1810. In that case Marshall, employing the legal fiction of an implied contract and the concept of property as a natural right, invalidated a state law as impairing the obligation of contracts even though the entire nation knew that the grant of land annulled by that law was based on fraud. But the interpretation of national policy on which this doctrine was grounded stems from forces creating the Ordinance of 1787, not from the opposing democratic spirit that Jefferson gave to that of 1784.

Thus in these formative years of the young nation and of his own career, Marshall took the path that led him to prefer order, stability, and a narrow application of those "principles of natural justice and social policy" in defense of property and contractual rights. . . . He came more and more to associate republicanism in America with revolutionary excesses in France, to identify the spirit of change and innovation with "the fatal philosophy of the day," and to personify these in the figure of one he spoke of derisively as "the great Lama of the Mountain." Toward the end he felt that the nation could scarcely survive such tendencies. "The union has been prolonged thus far by miracles," he wrote to Joseph Story in 1832. "I fear they cannot continue."

Jefferson entertained no such fears. He steadily maintained the path of nationalism on which he had set out in the beginning, regarding this as being along the common highway that belonged not to this nation alone but to all men. The contest for the improvement of the condition of man was to him not merely an acceptance of the idea of change but also a commitment to the task of bringing change about. His was a realistic and a pragmatic experimentalism, and he saw with Bacon that improvement in the condition of society presupposed improvement in the mind of man. "To be really useful," he wrote in 1807, "we must keep pace with the state of society, and not dishearten it by attempts at what it's population, means, or occupations will fail in attempting." But nothing in the spirit of the American people gave him greater confidence in the vitality of the nation and the stability of its institutions than the spirit of innovation. When in 1784 he drafted a report sustaining the authority of the national government as final and conclusive in the most difficult role a federative body could perform—that of acting as arbiter between two states of the union in a matter of vital importance to both—it was quite characteristic that he should see the example as one of universal applicability. "Perhaps," he declared for the benefit of a European audience, "history cannot produce such another proof of the empire of reason and right in any part of the world as these new states now exhibit. Other nations have only been able to submit private contests to judiciary determination; but these new states have gone further. They have . . . by wise and just arrangements submitted the causes of Nations to be weighed in the scales of justice by a tribunal so constituted as to ensure the confidence of all parties and so supported by the rest of the Union as to secure the execution of its decisions." The acquiescence in the federal determination of the jurisdictional claims of two states was by no means so submissive as Jefferson indicated, but even the exaggeration suggests that what he valued most was the innovative example in government set by the new world before the eyes of the old. This to him was evidence of a spirit in the people that had enabled them to achieve unprecedented heights in the development of their political institutions. The new federal constitution was a great new summit in this progressive experimentation. . . .

Marshall and Jefferson—kinsmen, products of the Virginia Piedmont, students of the law under George Wythe—became inexorable protagonists of two opposed views of man and society. Perhaps because of this similarity of background, each mistook the aim of the other. Marshall mistakenly thought Jefferson hostile to the idea of an independent judiciary, and believed this hostility to be in fact part of "a deep design to convert our government into a mere league of states." Jefferson thought that under Marshall the judiciary was "ever acting with noiseless foot and unalarming advance, gaining ground step by step, and . . . engulfing insidiously the special governments into the jaws of that which feeds them." These fears found reflection in words and in official acts, each man expressing his natural preference for the concerns that to him seemed most vital. Those dominant in the attitude of Marshall clustered about the rights of property and those that Jefferson placed first involved the rights of man. . . .

In his greatest decision Marshall voiced the view that the Constitution was intended to endure for ages to come and to be adaptable to the various crises of human affairs. But the whole tenor of his judicial thought was at variance with the philosophy thus expressed in his most viable and most enduring decision. Nothing is more surely demonstrable in the entire range of his decisions than his steady opposition to reformation, his intransigence in setting himself against the aspirations and needs of a growing people, his narrow interpretations of the broad grants of constitutional power in support of the confined interests of a special class. Imprisoned in his own allegiance to the Hamiltonian philosophy of government, Marshall thus becomes in the final analysis the strict constructionist, bound to the concepts of his own era. The rivets he employed to fasten in place what he regarded as the permanent elements of American constitutional law have in large part been replaced, and those he used to fix the role of the judiciary in the federal system would indubitably have been driven at their appointed time in any event. The partisan use of the judiciary that he feared under Jefferson was indeed an approximation of what had actually occurred under the first Federalist administrations. The glint of partisan prejudice was by no means absent from the Marshall court itself.

Jefferson's role thus becomes the opposite of that so long assigned him. Marshall's absolutes, including the concept of property as a natural right, have become less tenable and his figure has receded into the background. Jefferson's relativism, which embraced that feature of his thought that Marshall found most abhorrent, makes him seem at home in a wholly different age. But it was not Jefferson's conception of the changeableness of all laws and constitutions or even his persistent effort to promote conditions congenial to reformation that makes him enduringly relevant. It was rather the steadfast devotion with which he clung to his one absolute and gave it precedence over all others. "Nothing, then," he declared toward the end, "is unchangeable but the inherent and unalienable rights of man."

The significance of the implacable hostility between Marshall and Jefferson lies in the fact that, when one was Chief Justice and the other President, there came about the first elevated, informed discussion of the role of the judiciary. Marshall did not generate the profound and widespread resentment against partisan uses of the courts but neither did his decisions or his political attitudes tend to alleviate fears. . . .

To Jefferson the most cherished element of the Constitution was the Bill of Rights. This had been flagrantly violated by the Alien and Sedition Acts, with the tame and at times eager acquiescence of the judiciary. This overarching threat to a free press and to the right of the opposition to be heard had in fact been largely responsible for bringing Jefferson from retirement to a position of power. Under his leadership the nation had been unified and the opposition had been given a mortal wound. His party was not merely triumphant but was clamoring for curbs to put an end to judicial partisanship. Another Chief Magistrate in such circumstances, under the influence of a monumental enmity existing between him and the Chief Justice, might well have reached for one of the weapons that Marshall thought Jefferson intended to use. But respect for the independence of the judiciary and an understanding of its importance in a government of checks and balances—these enduring convictions rather than personal animus guided Jefferson's hand in this first great crisis over the judiciary. . . .

19

Adrienne Koch: "Take Care of Me When Dead"

Once Madison was freed from the burdens of office, Jefferson was the first to greet him as a long-absent voyager, home at last.[1] "I sincerely congratulate you." Jefferson wrote feelingly, "on your release from incessant labors, corroding anxieties, active enemies & interested friends, &, on your return to your books & farm to tranquility & independence. A day of these is worth ages of the former. But all this you know." . . .

Already Jefferson had plans on foot to draw Madison . . . into an important educational project—the founding of a university that would establish, Jefferson hoped, science and intellectual freedom beyond the level of any other American institution. "The good Old Dominion, the blessed mother of us all," he wrote to fellow Virginians, "will then raise her head with pride among the nations, will present to them that splendor of genius which she has ever possessed, but has too long suffered to rest uncultivated and unknown, and will become a centre of ralliance to the States whose youth she has instructed, and, as it were, adopted."

The peculiar fascination that the dream of a university exercised over Jefferson was due not only to his long-cherished love of knowledge and the social arts, but to his conviction that freedom and enlightenment were essential to each other. Consequently, the university he wished to father would be dedicated to "the free range of mind." Madison shared this belief, and gave it pithy expression when he wrote, approving a system of general education in Kentucky: "What spectacle can be more edifying or more seasonable, than . . . Liberty & Learning, each leaning on the other for their mutual and surest support?" Thus when Jefferson drew Madison into the nine-year cycle of preparatory work to create the University of Virginia, and asked him to take over its direction after his death, the two friends were embarking upon

---

[1] From Adrienne Koch, *Jefferson and Madison: The Great Collaboration* (New York: Alfred A. Knopf, 1950), Chapter Nine, pp. 260–75; 279–84. Reprinted by permission of the author.

the last great work of their lives, their last significant partnership. . . .

Jefferson had prepared himself for his role as educational leader, not only by the studious habits of a lifetime, but by taking a few talented pupils under his wing, in an informal way, opening to them the resources of his unsurpassed library, guiding their plans for reading, lecturing on special subjects of interest, and infusing his own broad and sound philosophy of learning and life. In general, Jefferson's approach to education was sharply critical of the kind of "specialization" that precedes a general philosophical orientation in the realm of ideas. He vigorously stated his ideal of a philosophical approach to any chosen field in a letter to a promising student. "Nothing can be sounder than your view of the importance of laying a broad foundation in other branches of knowledge whereon to raise the superstructure of any particular science which one would chuse to profess with credit & usefulness. The lamentable disregard of this, since the revolution has filled our country with Blackstone lawyers, Sangrado physicians, a ranting clergy, & a lounging gentry, who render neither honor nor service to mankind, and when their country has occasion for scientific services, it looks for them in vain over its wide extended surface."

While the University of Virginia was the child of Jefferson's labor, Madison contributed far more to its creation than has been recognized. There was hardly a step Jefferson took without consultation with Madison. Measures and plans were discussed by the old friends in advance of presentation to the other members of the board. They shared the vicissitudes and strain of personally recruiting the faculty. They plotted together on ways and means of influencing members of the legislature to obtain appropriations for the first-rate construction called for by Jefferson's blueprint—a benign sort of plotting that unfortunately never brought large enough appropriations to ease the corroding worries of the two public-spirited friends.

Jefferson first enlisted Madison's aid in the battle over the location of the proposed university. Jefferson, who would supervise every detail of its physical construction, naturally wanted it within easy reach of Monticello. . . . Then in the fall of 1817 Jefferson borrowed from Madison a copy of Palladio's treatise on architecture and kept it for a year. . . . The buildings, already begun, were to benefit from Jefferson's use of this architectural treatise, with its descriptions of neoclassic colonnaded houses, its conception of a villa as a whole, organized throughout, in plan and elevation, according to rules that integrated it with the landscape. . . .

Madison was soon also introduced to the problem of recruiting the faculty. The expert Dr. Thomas Cooper would have set up a first-rate department of medicine and chemistry for the new university, but Jefferson had heard that Cooper had received more attractive offers to remain in Philadelphia at a greater salary than could be guaranteed by the new university. . . .

Jefferson's next move was to devise a plan to enlist the help of Dugald Stewart, the Scottish "common-sense" philosopher whom Jefferson had known in Paris, and whose work Jefferson ranked with the highest of the "experimental" philosophers—the only kind of philosopher that Jefferson considered valuable. Jefferson also enlisted other academic acquaintances in England, Scotland, and on the Continent. Madison's first response to these proposals was interesting. He suggested that he had heard that one English scholar Jefferson meant to appeal to was "unfriendly to the U.S." and that Stewart's aid would be preferable, "if as I presume his political feelings be not at variance with his philosophical dispositions." As early as this, in the complicated maneuver of finding a high-grade group of professors for the university, Jefferson and Madison touched the highly charged periphery where political convictions impinge on professional competence.

By the beginning of 1818 Jefferson had prepared a letter for the Virginia legislators, outlining the progress on the plans for the university, and disclosing his intention to seek for professors abroad, in order to secure a faculty of genuine intellectual distinction. He sent the letter, as he so often had done before, to Madison for perusal and criticism. . . .

Jefferson also asked Madison to read and revise his important "Rockfish report," in preparation for the meeting of the educators and legislators at Rockfish Gap. The report, which outlined the basic schools within the contemplated university, was not, Jefferson said, the kind he would propose "to an assembly of philosophers, who would require nothing but the table of professorships." He had endeavored to adapt it to the Virginia House of Delegates, he said, and had deliberately tried to catch "the floating body of doubtful and wavering men" by throwing in leading ideas on the uses of education "in the hope that some of these might catch on some crotchet in their mind, and bring them over to us." Jefferson also apologized for having had to include sections on the general system of primary and secondary schools preliminary to the university. Madison was asked to revise the report in the light of these limiting circumstances. . . .

So hard did Jefferson work on the university project, personally supervising the construction, ordering the materials, revising his fundraising plans, and keeping accounts, as well as continuing with faculty procurement, that his health suffered. . . .

Jefferson did not spare himself from the exacting and exciting last job to which he had given himself, because he held that education was the greatest of all human causes as it was the indispensable road to liberty. . . . "What object of our lives can we propose so important? What interest of our own which ought not to be postponed to this? Health, time, labor, on what in the single life which nature has given us, can these be better bestowed than on this immortal boon to our country. The exertions and the mortifications are temporary; the benefit eternal." He then added, referring to his own labors, as he almost never did: "If any member of our college of visitors could justifiably withdraw from this sacred duty, it would be myself, who . . . have neither vigor of body nor mind left to keep the field; but I will die in the last ditch. . . ."

The more the buildings took shape and piecemeal grants for the university were made by the legislature, the more confident did Jefferson become about obtaining all the desired facilities. By the fall of 1821 he began discussing with Madison the cost of the excellent library he wished to provide for the university. He revealed his general philosophy: to make the total plan and construction of the university as complete as possible, and as excellent. "The world will never bear to see the doors of such an establishment locked up." This kind of gambling courage, necessary in good causes as well as selfish ones, carried through Jefferson's ideal of a university, despite the repeated obstacles he had to meet and overcome. His policy was firm: "Our course is a plain one, to pursue what is best, and the public will come right and approve us in the end." . . .

By 1823, when Jefferson had become an octogenarian, it was essential that he conserve his time for his majestic educational enterprise. Savage demands were being made upon both ex-Presidents for replies to letters from friends, acquaintances, and unknown thousands of citizens seeking intellectual, moral, or political advice. At the beginning of 1823 Jefferson asked Madison to reply to a friend who had asked for Jefferson's views on the forthcoming presidential election. "It is impossible for me to write to him with two crippled hands. I abandon writing but from the most urgent necessities; and above all things I should not meddle in a Presidential election, nor even express a sentiment on the subject of the Candidates." The "most urgent necessities" were a small circle of old friends, Madison foremost among them; and the university. Nor could Jefferson and Madison remain immune to queries that affected the fundamental political principles of their own lives. These letters the two aged statesmen felt impelled to scrutinize with their usual keen critical intelligence. They supplied answers breathing the ripe wisdom of long experience.

In the fall of 1823 Jefferson thought it time to dispatch an agent to Great Britain to procure the indispensable professors—with the exception of a law professor, whom Jefferson and Madison agreed would have to be a native American. Francis Walker Gilmer, himself a talented legal scholar, received this unique commission to the "republic of letters" in England and Scotland. . . .

At last Jefferson was able to write that the academic problem was temporarily solved. "Gilmer is arrived in New York. . . . He has engaged 5 Professors. . . ."

With a nucleus of foreign professors safely secured, a fresh problem arose—the choice of an appropriate professor of ethics. Jefferson considered ethics an indispensable part of general education, but hated to have it emerge in the distorted forms of authoritarian morality to which the clergy normally confined it. He was determined not to allow a clergyman to take over the teaching of moral philosophy, and preferred to see a well-educated and brilliant layman in charge of this controversial subject. He argued: "it is a branch of science of little difficulty to any ingenious man. Locke, Stewart, Brown, Tracy, for the general science of mind furnish materials abundant, and that of Ethics is still more trite. I should think any person with a general education rendering them otherwise worthy of a place among his scientific brethren might soon qualify himself." He suggested a young man formerly a student at William and Mary, who had been later educated at Edinburgh, and was considered one of the most distinguished American students ever there. The significance of this candidate proposed by Jefferson is that Jefferson put his faith in the Scottish school of common-sense empiricist philosophy in preference to the more metaphysical variety of philosophy then fashionable at Oxford and Cambridge.

In negotiating for native talent, Jefferson and Madison encountered an obstacle that has plagued American education ever since: "the difficulty in our country of withdrawing talents from rival pursuits into the service of Education." A long chase for a native professor of law, of ethics, and of literature brought home this truth with uncomfortable insistence to the eager founders of the University of Virginia. It also inadvertently forced to a head the issue of academic freedom and correctness of political principles in an institution that Madison had thought of as a future "nursery of Republican patriots as well as genuine scholars."

The search for an adequate law professor, after Gilmer declined the professorship, generated delicate questions of how far tolerance should go concerning the political beliefs of the prospective faculty. At first Jefferson only confessed his fears that they might hire "a mere Gothic lawyer who has no idea beyond his Coke Littleton, who could not associate in conversation with his Colleagues, nor utter a single Academical idea to an enquiring stranger." Jefferson, as he revealed in this value judgment, abhorred the tribe of narrow, pedantic scholars and expected philosophical awareness and breadth of interest as well as European conversational ease from the hand-picked professors. In recommending a candidate, Madison described him as a "convert to the constitutionality of canals. In other respects he adhered, I *believe*, to the Virginia Creed of which he had been a warm advocate. What his political sentiments are at present I know not." The issue was now out in the open. Jefferson, one of the few surviving "Argonauts" of 1776, and Madison, the dominating spirit of the Constitution, were unwilling to allow the entry of political doctrines contradictory to the cherished freedoms of democratic society and Republican ideology. . . .

In the late spring of 1824 Jefferson had begun to work on a book catalogue for the library of the university, devoting four hours a day to it for the period of two months and the entire day for several additional months. He told Madison he had undertaken to make out the catalogue because he had in his possession "a collection of excellent catalogues, and knowing no one capable, to whom we could refer the task. It has been laborious far beyond my expectation . . . and not yet in sight of the end. It will enable us to judge what the object will cost."

Jefferson's fascination with books had never deserted him. He had sold his first great library to the United States, to form the nucleus of the library of Congress, after the British had burned the national library in 1814. Jefferson had instantly begun to collect another library for himself after the last shipment of books had gone to Washington. This library was willed to the University of Virginia, but it was necessary for the family to sell most of it at auction instead, to pay part of the debt on Jefferson's estate. In any event, it was inconceivable that Jefferson would assign this task, always partly a labor of love, to anyone else. . . .

Fortunately, the University was opening. Students were coming by the Richmond and Fredericksburg stages as far as they could, and hiring horses when those got stuck in the unpassable roads. Books had not yet arrived for the young men, but the electric atmosphere of a new educational world was beginning to be felt. A law professor, John

Tayloe Lomax, recommended by Madison's friend Judge Barbour, was appointed, after determining that he had "extended his studies beyond the ordinary municipal law, to the law of nations and to the more philosophical view of the general subjects." The "bantling of forty years' growth and nursing" was about to take its place in the world.

The following year found Jefferson convinced that he would soon "remove beyond the reach of attentions to the University, or beyond the bourne of life itself"; and he wrote to Madison committing the university to his care in that event, and professing ardently the joy and satisfaction he had received from this friendship of half a century.

Bewilderingly heavy financial difficulties had arisen for Jefferson to disturb his last months with agonizing worries about the fate of his family's resources. He petitioned to sell his lands at public lottery, retaining only Monticello itself. The purpose of the lottery was to obtain better prices than the depreciated land value at the time would have netted in an ordinary sale—a purpose, unfortunately, that was not realized. These troubles he confided to Madison, who was himself in hard-pressed circumstances and who foresaw a similar end for his own estate. Jefferson did not like to afflict others with his troubles, and indeed he had been singularly adequate to all of life's burdens in his long career. But, he confessed, "pains are lessened by communication with a friend."

It was on this occasion that Jefferson stated, once in his life, the luminous truth that had been the source of so much consolation to him throughout his active life and in the retirement that, despite its many afflictions, had been made rich and happy. "The friendship which has subsisted between us, now half a century," Thomas Jefferson wrote to James Madison, "and the harmony of our political principles and pursuits, have been sources of constant happiness to me through that long period. . . . Take care of me when dead, and be assured that I shall leave with you my last affections." . . .

It was late in the day for Jefferson to go against the grain, changing the habits of his long and good life. At the end of the following month he was gravely ill. On the 1st of July, Madison had a note from Dr. Dunglison referring to the danger of Jefferson's condition. And on the 4th of July, on the fiftieth anniversary of the Declaration of Independence, Thomas Jefferson died.

The generous spirit that had animated Jefferson's work and life was kept alive by Madison in his role of spiritual guardian of his friend's reputation. The care of the University of Virginia, which had been placed in his hands, was conscientiously accepted. At the sacrifice of health and the precious time that remained, Madison took on the thankless duties for eight years after Jefferson's death. Though he could hardly afford it, he gave the university pecuniary aid, and provided, in a codicil to his will, a bequest of needed books that his library could supply. He could not allow himself proper credit, tendered by friends, for his work as rector of the university, so anxious was he to have the world remember Jefferson as its creator and creative genius. In summing up the work his dearest friend had put into it, Madison himself became eloquent. "The University of Virginia, as a temple dedicated to science and liberty, was, after his retirement from the political sphere, the object nearest his heart, and so continued to the close of his life. His devotion to it was intense, and his exertions unceasing. It bears the stamp of his genius, and will be a noble monument of his fame." . . .

Afterword

To borrow a thought from Albert Schweitzer's book, *The Quest for the Historical Jesus,* one knows with certainty that whatever happens to change American life and destinies, the search for the historical Jefferson will not cease. This great philospher–statesman, the butt for his detractors' dirt and the inspiration for the people's hopes, will continue to enrich the historical imagination of each successive age. Even the ritualistic annihilations that attempt periodically to peck out his eyes are not likely to do their intended work. John Adams knew: "Thomas Jefferson still survives," the old man said, in his last whispered words. Why so? We must resort to the wisdom of Jefferson's great modern editor, Julian Boyd, for the answer. Jefferson's genius is bound up with "the most potent idea of modern history, as valid for the twentieth century as for the eighteenth"— the idea of freedom and self-government for all mankind. One need only muse: what would American history have been without the spirit, the "electric cord" of Jefferson's ideas and words to unite it in fellowship with the hopes of men and women in all lands, under any sky? *Without* Jefferson, America would have had a history, but of another sort; a civilization too, no doubt, but without the radiance and the power of renewal to emerge from mistaken by-ways and find again its central path.

"Everyman" is doubtless free to try to be "his own Jeffersonian." But Jefferson was not a thing of wax. Like his great predecessor, and good friend, the unforgettable Dr. Franklin, the simple tribute "Vir" can not be erased from his reality. That is why Americans have fought for the protection, sometimes merely the protective coloration, of his mantle. But while common sense, good humor, and a passionate capacity for seeking truth and expressing it winningly remain in short supply, Jefferson will ever be the magnanimous man to whom Americans return for examples of insight and personal courage.

That one so peculiarly American, and intimately a Virginian, should have the power to communicate with all mankind seems improbable. Yet the liberal royalist, Mounier, seeking advice before the opening meeting of the National Assembly, repaired to Jefferson's home in Paris in the summer of 1789, wanting (in his own words) to consult "an American, known for his lights and his virtues, who had together at once the experience and the theory of the appropriate institutions to maintain liberty." Mounier failed to learn the secret, but others turned up, and will do so again, for another try. Seven years after Jefferson's death Sainte Beuve advised: "Read and read again Jefferson." He urged his readers to learn from Jefferson "the lesson." And what was that? "For the liberty and the diversity of human minds is both the most inescapable and the most respectable fact henceforth to be considered in dealing with the problem of human society." Of course, contemporary with the man who so admonished his readers, were others like George Fitzhugh, author of an incitatory tract appropriately entitled *Cannibals All,* who pictured Jefferson as "the architect of ruin, the inaugurator of anarchy." He too would have descendants, but Jefferson could not be downed.

The time came for the modern world to reconsider human rights and the unquenchable desire for freedom. What did it take? From India, Mahatma Gandhi wrote a significant message to the Director of UNESCO. "I learned from my illiterate but wise mother that all rights to be deserved and preserved came from duty well done. Thus, the very right to live accrues to us only when we do the duty of citizenship of the world. From this one fundamental statement, perhaps it is easy enough to define duties of Man and Woman and correlate every right to some corresponding duty to be first performed. Every other right can be shown to be a usurpation hardly worth fighting for." This was a Jeffersonian message, in a vast, new, and awesome world. Modern cynics have presented Jefferson as a child of light, unaware of the darker side of human suffering and deception. On the contrary, knowing the evil that men do, and the creatureliness of man's condition, Jefferson would not yield to fear. The last book he read was found on his bedside night table by his young relative, Nicholas P. Trist. It was written by the Stoic philosopher, Seneca. Fortitude, for the pursuit of happiness, was an old lesson Jefferson had learned from the legacy of antiquity when he was a boy in his teens.

An exquisite life portrait of Jefferson as an old man was painted by Thomas Sully in 1821. It found its way to West Point, where it was viewed by James Fenimore Cooper, whose antipathies to Jefferson were well known. As he confronted the painting, Cooper requested his companion to wait. The companion testified that Cooper later "pronounced it one of the finest portraits he had ever beheld, and that he would never have forgiven me if I had let it escape his notice. But you will smile when I tell you its effects on myself. There was a dignity, a repose, I will go further and say a loveliness, about this painting, that I never have seen in any other portrait. . . . I saw . . .

Jefferson, standing before me, not in red breeches and slovenly attire, but a gentleman, appearing in all republican simplicity, with a grace and ease on the canvas, that to me seem unrivalled. It has really shaken my opinion of Jefferson as a man, if not as a politician; and when his image recurs to me now, it is in the simple robes of Sully, sans red breeches, or even without any of the repulsive accompaniments of a political 'sans culotte.' "

This kind of testimony from Jefferson's political *enemies* is all we can ask, and it is enough. Not many who have founded a nation and led a modern revolution could lay claim to a "loveliness" that transcends ideology and reminds posterity of the glory and dignity of the common human person.

Bibliographical Note

The splendid editorial enterprise of Julian Boyd, editor of *The Papers of Thomas Jefferson* (Princeton, 1950–) has already published eighteen volumes of the correspondence to and from Jefferson, and the documents which he wrote or drafted. These volumes are a treasure house of information not only about Thomas Jefferson—his ideas, doings, mode of expression, and method of conducting himself and public business—but of the formative period of the United States from revolutionary days to the early years of the republic under the Federal Constitution. The complete set of Jefferson's *Papers* will run to approximately fifty volumes. As each volume appears, a deepened and more reliable knowledge of Thomas Jefferson and the culture in which he flourished becomes available to the serious student of this great American philosopher-statesman.

For the years not yet covered by the Boyd edition, readers must resort to two older, inferior editions, one edited by Paul L. Ford, *The Writings of Thomas Jefferson,* 10 vols. (New York: G. P. Putnam's Sons, 1898–1899), the other edited by A. A. Lipscomb and A. E. Bergh, *The Writings of Thomas Jefferson,* 20 Vols. (Washington, D.C.: Thomas Jefferson Memorial Association of U.S., 1903).

A major and indispensable source of knowledge and interpretation of Jefferson is provided by Dumas Malone's multivolume biography, *Jefferson and His Time.* Four volumes of Mr. Malone's magnificent study have been published: *Jefferson the Virginian* (Boston: Little, Brown and Company, 1948); *Jefferson and the Rights of Man* (1951); *Jefferson and the Ordeal of Liberty* (1962); *Jefferson the President: First Term, 1801–1805* (1969). Mr. Malone's plan calls for two more volumes to complete this biography, which has already proven to be a pioneer work in unravelling the complex and hitherto inadequately known aspects of Jefferson's life.

For readers who desire a one-volume introduction to the writings of Jefferson, there is the Modern Library edition of *The Life and Selected Writings of Thomas Jefferson,* edited by Adrienne Koch and William Peden (New York: Randon House, Inc., 1944).

The complete correspondence between John Adams and Thomas Jefferson is available in two attractive volumes edited by Lester Cappon, *The Adams-Jefferson Letters* (Chapel Hill: University of North Carolina Press, 1959). For a brief study of this relationship, see Adrienne Koch, *Adams and Jefferson: Posterity Must Judge,* Berkeley Series in American History (Chicago: Rand McNally & Co., 1963). For the relationship between Jefferson and Madison see the same author's *Jefferson and Madison: The Great Collaboration* (New York: Oxford University Press, Inc., 1964), available in paperback. Jefferson's changing and multifaceted influence on American History from 1826 to our own times is the subject of Merril D. Peterson's *The Jefferson Image in the American Mind* (New York: Oxford University Press, Inc., 1960).

Index

GREAT LIVES OBSERVED

Gerald Emanuel Stearn, *General Editor*

Other volumes in the series:

Bismarck, *edited by Frederic B. M. Hollyday*

John C. Calhoun, *edited by Margaret L. Coit*

Churchill, *edited by Martin Gilbert*

Cromwell, *edited by Maurice Ashley*

Elizabeth I, *edited by Joseph M. Levine*

Frederick Douglass, *edited by Benjamin Quarles*

Frederick the Great, *edited by Louis L. Snyder*

Henry Ford, *edited by John B. Rae*

Garibaldi, *edited by Denis Mack Smith*

William Lloyd Garrison, *edited by George M. Frederickson*

Hitler, *edited by George H. Stein*

Jesus, *edited by Hugh Anderson*

La Follette, *edited by Robert S. Maxwell*

Lloyd George, *edited by Martin Gilbert*

Huey Long, *edited by Hugh Davis Graham*

Joseph R. McCarthy, *edited by Allen J. Matusow*

Mao, *edited by Jerome Ch'en*

Peter the Great, *edited by L. Jay Oliva*

Robespierre, *edited by George Rudé*

(continued on following page)

(continued from previous page)